LEARNING HOW TO LOVE WITH ST. THÉRÈSE

Learning How to Love *with* St. Thérèse

SEVEN WINDOWS INTO TRUE CHARITY

FR. JOSEPH SPENCE, FFM

Angelico Press

First published in the USA
by Angelico Press 2026

For information, address:
Angelico Press, Ltd.
169 Monitor St.
Brooklyn, NY 11222
www.angelicopress.com

ppr 979-8-89280-186-7
cloth 979-8-89280-187-4
ebook 979-8-89280-188-1

Book and cover design
by Michael Schrauzer

CONTENTS

ABBREVIATIONS

Writings and Sources of St. Thérèse of Lisieux

CJ — Carnet Jaune (*Yellow Notebook*) of Mother Agnes of Jesus, in St. Thérèse of Lisieux, *Her Last Conversations*, translated by John Clarke, O.C.D., Washington, D.C.: ICS Publications, 1977.

CSG — Conseils et Souvenirs *(Advice and Memoirs)* of Sr. Geneviève, in *My Sister St. Thérèse, by Sister Geneviève of the Holy Face (Celine Martin)*, authorized translation by the Carmelite Sisters of New York of *Conseils et Souvenirs*, Rockford, Illinois: TAN Books and Publishers, 1997.

LT — Letters from Thérèse, in St. Thérèse of Lisieux, *General Correspondence: Volume I (1877–1890)*, translated by John Clarke, O.C.D., Washington D.C.: ICS Publications, 1982; St. Thérèse of Lisieux, *General Correspondence: Volume II (1890–1897)*, translated by John Clarke, O.C.D., Washington, D.C.: ICS Publications, 1988.

Ms A — Manuscript A: Autobiographical manuscript dedicated to Mother Agnes of Jesus, in *Story of a Soul: The Autobiography of Saint Thérèse of Lisieux*, translated from the original manuscripts by John Clarke, O.C.D., a Study Edition prepared by Marc Foley, O.C.D., Washington, D.C.: ICS Publications, 2012.

Ms B — Manuscript B: Letter to Sr. Marie of the Sacred Heart, in *Story of a Soul: The Autobiography of Saint Thérèse of Lisieux*, translated from the original manuscripts by John Clarke, O.C.D., a Study Edition prepared by Marc Foley, O.C.D., Washington, D.C.: ICS Publications, 2012.

Ms C — Manuscript C: Autobiographical manuscript dedicated to Mother Marie de Gonzague, in *Story of a Soul: The Autobiography of Saint Thérèse of Lisieux*, translated from the original manuscripts by John Clarke, O.C.D., a Study Edition prepared by Marc Foley, O.C.D., Washington, D.C.: ICS Publications, 2012.

P — Poems of St. Thérèse of the Child Jesus, in *The Poetry of Saint Thérèse of Lisieux, Complete Edition: Texts and Introductions*, translated by Donald Kinney, O.C.D., Washington, D.C.: ICS Publications, 1996.

Pr Prayers of St. Thérèse of the Child Jesus, in *The Prayers of Saint Thérèse of Lisieux*, General Introduction by Guy Gaucher, O.C.D., translated by Aletheia Kane, O.C.D., Washington, D.C.: ICS Publications, 1997.

PR Pious Recreations of St. Thérèse of the Child Jesus, in *The Plays of Saint Thérèse of Lisieux: "Pious Recreations,"* General Introduction by Guy Gaucher, O.C.D., translated by Susan Conroy and David J. Dwyer, Washington, D.C.: ICS Publications, 2008.

FOREWORD

I met with Fr. Joseph Spence when he was still a student. In fact, I followed his doctoral thesis as his Professor (Co-Moderator). He wrote his doctorate on St. John of the Cross's influence on St. Thérèse of the Child Jesus and of the Holy Face. The Spanish mystic San Juan de la Cruz, protagonist in the reform of the Carmelite Order together with St. Teresa of Ávila, was in fact an important influence in St. Thérèse's life and spirituality. He educated the "spousal chord" of her heart. Her Divine Spouse, of course, was Jesus. When Thérèse spoke or wrote about God, she generally preferred to speak of Him with a name, the name of the Incarnate Word: *Jésus*.

Fr. Joseph then became a colleague of mine not only at the Pontifical Theological Faculty "*Teresianum*," but also at the Pontifical Athenaeum "*Regina Apostolorum*," both of which are located in Rome, Italy. I had the joy and the grace of teaching for a lifetime in both of these theological faculties. I was also asked, among other things, to be a theological consultant for the Congregation of the Causes of Saints, a precious service that I have gladly committed myself to for many years now, and continue to do so today. The object, in fact, of my research and teaching has always been prominently that of the "Theology of Saints." And St. Thérèse of Lisieux has been my preferred saint, among all.

It is with great joy, then, that I may now present to you readers this new publication on Thérèse's fraternal charity. Surprisingly enough, only one significant study has so far been done on this important aspect of Thérèse's experience. I'm referring to the book of the renowned scholar, Fr. Pierre Descouvemont, entitled *Thérèse de Lisieux et son prochain* (*Thérèse of Lisieux and her Neighbor*). Although an important book, published in the year 2003, it has remained the only one on the topic; and, unfortunately, it has not—as of yet—been translated into English.

Fr. Joseph has approached the subject from a different point of view. The renowned Theresian scholar, Fr. Descouvemont, examined the topic from five perspectives, which correspond to the five chapters of his book: "Give thanks for one's neighbor," "Love God above all," "Love one's neighbor for love of God," "Love one's neighbor with Jesus's heart," and "Return to earth after death." Fr. Joseph privileged a different standpoint. He preferred focusing, rather, on the people whom Thérèse herself loved, with the love of Jesus. Therefore, his book comprises nine chapters, focusing specifically on seven of the most important "categories" of people whom Thérèse loved.

After a brief introduction to Thérèse's life experience (first chapter), Fr. Joseph clarifies the deep connection between love for God and neighbor that animated Thérèse's fraternal charity (second chapter). He then proceeds (from chapters 3–9) to explore all of those persons whom Thérèse herself loved so dearly, and with a heroic Christian charity: her family members, sinners, priests, her fellow sisters in the monastery, holy souls in Purgatory and in Heaven, her spiritual sons and daughters, and all men and women of all time.

This broad overview and vision of Thérèse's fraternal charity—Thérèse, in fact, had a very ample vision of the faith and of the Church—is supplemented and nourished, in Fr. Joseph's book, from various sources. Not only does he draw abundantly from her *Writings*, including her *Manuscripts* A, B, and C (*Story of a Soul*), her *Letters*, her *Poems*, her *Plays*, and her *Prayers*; but he also relies on other primary and important sources of her time: in particular, the testimonies of those who knew Thérèse, gathered at the Ordinary and Apostolic Processes for her Beatification and Canonization. Occurrences in Thérèse's lifetime and family enrich the context and provide the "frame," as it were, for the "picture" that Fr. Joseph paints us of Thérèse's wonderful and inspiring fraternal charity.

In a world today, so needy of fraternal bonds, forgiveness, and selfless love—when all seems to point in other directions—Thérèse's gestures and words provide a stark contrast, together with a luminous example. If all were to imitate Jesus, or rather, receive and assimilate His love, even up to "laying down one's life for one's friends" (cf. Jn 15:13)—as Jesus did for us—and as Thérèse so well understood and put into practice... Well, the world would be a different place.

May Thérèse take us by hand and lead us into a deeper and ever-more convinced *sequela Christi*, so that the greeting of peace (*Pax vobis*) may resonate throughout the world today. My congratulations to Fr. Joseph for this timely and needed publication: timely and needed, I say, in a world where fraternal charity seems to be on the bottom of the priority list. May it rise to the top, and may this book be one tiny step closer to such a noble goal.

March 1st, 2026
Fr. François-Marie Léthel, O.C.D.

INTRODUCTION

In a world torn by war and hatred, by mistrust and prejudices between peoples and institutions, where can one turn for a message of hope, of love, of fraternity? How can one put into practice Jesus's teachings in the Gospel; what examples and witnesses can we find in our modern-day world of His message of love and forgiveness? How can one love his neighbor, above and beyond feelings of natural antipathy? Is it possible to love another with an unconditional love, and to freely give one's time, patience, and—why not?—one's best smile, to those whom one is not naturally attracted to?

Certainly, "the greatest saint of modern times," as Pope Pius X defined Thérèse of Lisieux not long after her death, can come to our aid . . . In the past century after St. Pius X's prophetic statement, the Church and the world have proposed Thérèse over and over again, as a cultural and spiritual model for humanity. On October 19th, 1997, St. John Paul II proclaimed Thérèse a "Doctor of the Church."[1] Moreover, the *United Nations Educational, Scientific, and Cultural Organization* (UNESCO) recognized Thérèse as a "World Heritage Person" on occasion of the 150th anniversary of her birth; for the same occasion—that is, for the 150th anniversary of Thérèse's birth—Pope Francis promulgated his Apostolic Exhortation *C'est la confiance*, entirely dedicated to Thérèse and her spiritual message.[2] The year 2025 was, furthermore, the Centenary of her Canonization (May 17th, 1925).

---

[1] See the Apostolic Letter of His Holiness Pope John Paul II, *Divini Amoris Scientia*, https://www.vatican.va/content/john-paul-ii/en/apost_letters/1997/documents/hf_jp-ii_apl_19101997_divini-amoris.html (accessed on April 1st, 2025).

[2] Cf. the Apostolic Exhortation *C'est la confiance* of the Holy Father Francis on Confidence in the Merciful Love of God for the 150th Anniversary of the Birth of St. Thérèse of the Child Jesus and the Holy Face, https://www.vatican.va/content/francesco/en/apost_exhortations/documents/20231015-santateresa-delbambinogesu.html (accessed on April 1st, 2025).

Besides her "Little Way," one of the most striking messages of Thérèse is precisely her fraternal charity. Surprisingly enough, literature in that regard is almost void. Those who have not entered into the world of studies regarding St. Thérèse might think that so many books have been written on her, that nothing else is left to be studied or talked about. Thankfully, that opinion is erroneous. One example will suffice: besides a few articles, which of course are incomplete, only one book has been written on the topic of Thérèse's fraternal charity; I'm referring to Fr. Pierre Descouvemont's *Thérèse de Lisieux et son prochain.*[3] (In English: *Thérèse of Lisieux and her Neighbor.*) Unfortunately, this study of Fr. Descouvemont—an expert on Thérèse—is only available in French.

Twenty-three years after the publication of *Thérèse de Lisieux et son prochain*, in the light of the recent proclamations regarding Thérèse, and considering the recent wars and conflicts that continue to lacerate peoples and humanity, it seems opportune to present Thérèse's experience of fraternal charity with more force and clarity than ever. I've chosen a completely different style and approach than that of Descouvemont's. I did so for two reasons: first of all, to not risk to be repetitive; second of all—but more importantly—I feel that Thérèse's experience and *Writings* have even more to offer. I've tried to let Thérèse "speak for herself," in such a way that her own *Writings*, the happenings of her life, and the testimonies of those who knew her and experienced her fraternal charity on a personal level, could speak more clearly and more strongly than any re-interpretation or theological re-elaboration of her message.

Without further ado, then, let us open our eyes to contemplate, and our ears to listen, once more—almost like those privileged contemporaries of Thérèse—her exquisite and heroic charity toward her neighbor. Thérèse's fraternal

[3] P. Descouvemont, *Thérèse de Lisieux et son prochain* (Paris: Les Éditions du Cerf, 2003).

charity, after all, is the true counterproof of her ardent charity toward God, according to that two-fold and inseparable commandment that Jesus Himself declared:

> Hearing that Jesus had silenced the Sadducees, the Pharisees got together. One of them, an expert in the law, tested him with this question: "Teacher, which is the greatest commandment in the Law?"
>
> Jesus replied: "'Love the Lord your God with all your heart and with all your soul and with all your mind.' This is the first and greatest commandment. And the second is like it: 'Love your neighbor as yourself.' All the Law and the Prophets hang on these two commandments" (Mt 22:34–40).

ST. THÉRÈSE AT THIRTEEN YEARS OF AGE (FEBRUARY 1886)[1]

[1] For the photos regarding St. Thérèse of the Child Jesus and of the Holy Face contained in this study, please refer to the Carmel of Lisieux Archives Website, at: https://archives.carmeldelisieux.fr/en/ (accessed on April 1st, 2025).

FIRST CHAPTER

St. Thérèse's Spiritual Journey: A Biographical Overview

INTRODUCTION: THÉRÈSE'S FIRST STEPS IN THIS WORLD

Our dear St. Thérèse was the last of nine children, born of Sts. Louis and Zélie Martin; and here are the names of their children: Marie-Louise (Sr. Mary of the Sacred Heart); Marie-Pauline (Mother Agnès of Jesus); Marie-Léonie (Sr. Françoise-Thérèse); Marie-Hélène; Marie-Joseph Louis; Marie Joseph Jean-Baptiste; Marie-Céline (Sr. Geneviève of the Holy Face); Marie-Mélanie Thérèse; Marie-Françoise Thérèse (St. Thérèse of the Child Jesus and of the Holy Face).[2] Four of these nine children died at a tender age.

Marie-Françoise Thérèse Martin was, thus, born on January 2nd, 1873, in Alençon, France, at 11:30 PM. While in the womb, Zélie had thought that Thérèse was a boy! The strength of Thérèse's character will later shine forth, most especially in the last years of her brief earthly existence. Two days after her birth, Thérèse was baptized.[3] Although stronger than her siblings, Thérèse was struggling for life. The enteritis—that is, inflammation of the small intestine—that had taken the life of her deceased brothers and sisters now threatened her own. There was only one solution: bring her to Zélie's trusted wet nurse, Rose Taillé, eight kilometers away, in the countryside. Thérèse was saved! And she would remain with her wet nurse for an entire year—actually, for fifteen months—before returning to Alençon. In the meantime, visits from her parents and sisters were frequent.

---

[2] See 5–7 of "*Detailed Genealogy*," available in the "*Genealogy of the Martins and Guérins*" Section, under the "*Family Environment*" tab of the Carmel of Lisieux Archives online: https://archives.carmeldelisieux.fr/wp-content/uploads/2022/08/genealogieSteTherese.pdf (accessed on April 1st, 2025).

[3] Cf. G. Gaucher, *Saint Thérèse of Lisieux: The Story of a Life* (San Francisco, CA: Ignatius Press, 2019), 15.

Thérèse's infancy in her new and true home in Alençon was full of love and happiness, surrounded by her affectionate family.[4] The little "imp" Thérèse, as her mother Zélie called her, offers a sort of "self-portrait" with her first *Letter*, written with the help of her elder sister Pauline on April 4th, 1877. The evening before, Thérèse had told Pauline that she wanted to become a "religious in a cloister."[5] Guided by Pauline's hand, Thérèse herself wrote to Louise:

> Dear little Louise,
>
> I don't know you, but I love you very much just the same. Pauline told me to write you: she is holding me on her knees because I don't know how to hold a pen. She wants me to tell you that I'm a lazy little girl, but this isn't true because I work all day long playing tricks on my poor little sisters. So I'm a little rascal who is always laughing. *Adieu*, little Louise. I'm sending you a big kiss [...] (LT 1).

HER MOTHER ZÉLIE'S SICKNESS AND DEATH

The innocent bliss of Thérèse's infancy, revealed in these few lines of her first *Letter*, was about to come to an end. Her mother Zélie, unbeknownst to the little one, had been diagnosed in December 1876 with a "fibrous tumour" in her breast that was "no use operating."[6] Zélie went in pilgrimage to Lourdes to ask the Blessed Virgin Mary for a miraculous cure. It was to no avail..."If the Blessed Mother does not cure me it's because my time is at an end, and God wants me to rest elsewhere other than on earth,"[7] Zélie wrote to her brother Isidore. On August 28th, 1877, Thérèse's mother

---

[4] See Gaucher, *Saint Thérèse of Lisieux: The Story of a Life*, 22–23.

[5] See St. Thérèse of Lisieux, *General Correspondence*, vol. 1 (1887–1890), transl. John Clarke, O.C.D. (Washington, D.C.: ICS Publications, 2014), 108–9.

[6] Cf. Gaucher, *Saint Thérèse of Lisieux: The Story of a Life*, 31.

[7] See the Archives of the Carmel of Lisieux website, under the tab "Family Environment—Correspondence"; "Filter by senders—Zélie Guérin," on the date August 16th, 1877, https://archives.carmeldelisieux.fr/en/correspondance/de-mme-martin-a-son-frere-isidore-guerin-cf-217-16-aout-1877/ (accessed on April 1st, 2025).

Zélie passed away. Thérèse was four years old. She describes her mother's death with gloomy notes in her *Manuscript* A: "All the details of my mother's illness are still present to me and I recall especially the last weeks she spent on earth [...]. The day of Mama's departure or the day after, Papa took me in his arms and said: 'Come, kiss your poor little mother for the last time'" (Ms A, 12r°).

ST. ZÉLIE MARTIN (THÉRÈSE'S MOTHER)

THE AFTERMATH OF ZÉLIE'S DEATH

This unhappy turn of events would deeply affect the suddenly fragile psyche of the *petite Thérèse*. For the next ten years of her life, Zélie's death would resound in Thérèse's subconsciousness causing a profound change in her personality. The outgoing, babbly, cheerful, and care-free baby Thérèse suddenly became overly sensitive and shy.

Louis Martin, Thérèse's father—now a widower—readily accepted the advice of Isidore Guérin, Zélie's brother: he must move to Lisieux together with his five daughters, to be closer to family. Thérèse later wrote, "I experienced no regret whatsoever at leaving Alençon; children are fond of change, and it was with pleasure that I came to Lisieux" (Ms A, 13v°). The hustle and bustle of Zélie's at-home business in lace-making, at Alençon, gave way to a quiet and almost "monastic" lifestyle in their new home, a lovely brick house on the fringes of Lisieux, called *Les Buissonnets*.[8] And so, two years quickly passed by, until a very significant event was to come about in little Thérèse's life: her first Confession. Thérèse would later write, "Coming out of the confessional I was so happy and light-hearted that I had never felt so much joy in my soul."

Apart from the normal trials of everyday life, the first three years at *Les Buissonnets* impressed happy memories in Thérèse. At least in part, her sisters' and her dear father's affection and tenderness substituted the lack of her mother Zélie. This happy and sheltered atmosphere, however, was not destined to last forever:[9] Thérèse had to start going to school. Thérèse was, at that point, eight years old. She would later write: "I have often heard it said that the time spent at school is the best and happiest of one's life. It wasn't this way for me. The five years I spent in school were the saddest in my life" (Ms A, 22r°).

THE "LOSS" OF PAULINE; A "STRANGE SICKNESS"; A MIRACULOUS CURE

Besides school, which was quite an emotional burden on the child, another strife was looming on the horizon, another loss: this time, it would prove to be too much for Thérèse, bringing her to a profound emotional and psychological instability.[10] With Pauline's entrance into Carmel, Thérèse suddenly

---

[8] See Gaucher, *Saint Thérèse of Lisieux: The Story of a Life*, 42–43.

[9] Cf. ibid., 47.

[10] See ibid., 52–53.

lost her "second mother," whom she had chosen for herself the very day of her mother Zélie's funeral . . . In the midst of this extreme anguish, however, the Holy Spirit was at work: when thinking over what Pauline had told her about life in the Carmel, Thérèse felt that "Carmel was the *desert* where God wanted me to go also to hide myself." Notwithstanding the peace in her soul, and the "certitude of a divine call" to Carmel, Thérèse's fragile psyche could no longer bear another loss as important as that of Pauline. Psychosomatic symptoms were not long in coming . . . and, as time passed, Thérèse's condition did not ameliorate—on the contrary. A true miracle was necessary. *Petite Thérèse* was close to death. A novena of Masses was offered at Our Lady of Victories, a Marian Shrine in Paris to whom the Martins and Guérins were particularly tied. On Pentecost Sunday, 1882, during the novena to Our Lady of Victories, there was an unexpected turn of events; Thérèse would later write about it:

> Finding no help on earth, poor little Thérèse had also turned toward the Mother of Heaven, and prayed with all her heart that she take pity on her. All of a sudden, the Blessed Virgin appeared *beautiful* to me, so *beautiful* that never had I seen anything so attractive; her face was suffused with an ineffable benevolence and tenderness, but what penetrated to the very depths of my soul was the *"ravishing smile of the Blessed Virgin."* At that instant, all my pain disappeared, and two large tears glistened on my eyelashes, and flowed down my cheeks silently, but they were tears of unmixed joy (Ms A, 30r°–30v°).

Thérèse was cured! I would say, miraculously cured. She resumed her everyday life the day after, and had no significant relapses afterward.

THÉRÈSE'S FIRST COMMUNION (MAY 8TH, 1884) AND HER "CONVERSION" ON CHRISTMAS EVE, 1886

After summer vacations, school at the Benedictine Abbey began once more. It was the school year of 1883–1884, and was to be the year of Thérèse's First Communion! We can "steal" a "glimpse" of Thérèse's experience from her recount of her First Communion, received on May 8th, 1884. She wrote:

> Ah! how sweet was that first kiss of Jesus! It was a kiss of love; I *felt* that *I was loved*, and I said: "I love You, and I give myself to You forever!" There were no demands made, no struggles, no sacrifices; for a long time now Jesus and poor little Thérèse *looked* at and understood each other. That day, it was no longer simply a *look*, it was a fusion; they were no longer two, Thérèse had vanished as a drop of water is lost in the immensity of the ocean (Ms A, 35r°).

As I wrote in my doctoral thesis on Thérèse's spousal experience, and St. John of the Cross's influence upon her, Thérèse's First Communion is probably the first, most significant experience of her relationship with Jesus as Spouse.[11] Only five weeks later, on June 14th, 1884, Thérèse received another important Sacrament: her Holy Confirmation. Thérèse would later describe the sacrament of Confirmation as the "Sacrament of Love" (Ms A, 36v°). "On that day," Thérèse continued, "I received the strength to *suffer*," for soon after the martyrdom of my soul was about to begin" (Ms A, 36v°–37r°). That is, Thérèse writes, "The terrible sickness of scruples" (Ms A, 39r°). This "martyrdom" was bound to last for a year and a half... After her bout of scruples had healed, Thérèse remained, however, overly sensitive: she was prone to get upset and cry far too much and too often. Who could heal Thérèse of her childish tears and faults? Who could fill in that void of affection and love, strength, and confidence, that had been lacking for Thérèse since her mother's sudden and tragic death?... Only the "*strong* and *powerful* God," as Thérèse would later describe Him. It was Christmas Eve, 1886. On that holy night, Thérèse found the strength to overcome her childish sentiments and master her

[11] Cf. J. Spence, *Un'esperienza sponsale con Dio: l'influsso di san Giovanni della Croce su santa Teresa di Lisieux* (tesi di dottorato), Pontificia Facoltà Teologica "*Teresianum*," Rome, 2020.

hurt feelings. You know the episode, so I won't describe it now. Thérèse would later write: "Thérèse had discovered once again the strength of soul which she had lost at the age of four and a half, and she was to preserve it forever" (Ms A, 45r°)! She also defined that moment as "the grace of my complete conversion" (cf. ibid.).

THE "THIRD PERIOD" OF THÉRÈSE'S LIFE

So was to begin the "third period" of Thérèse's life, according to she herself, "the most beautiful and the most filled with graces from Heaven" (cf. Ms A, 45v°). Thus began, as well, the year 1887, a fundamental year for Thérèse: a year of growth—physical, emotional, intellectual, and spiritual—and, also, the year in which she would mature her vocation and fight to achieve her goal: her entrance to Carmel.

The first step necessary for achieving her goal was to have her beloved father's permission. She chose Pentecost Sunday to "break the news." It was the twenty-ninth of May 1887.[12] It's best to leave the telling of this moving episode to Thérèse herself:

> Through my tears, I confided my desire to enter Carmel and soon his tears mingled with mine. He didn't say one word to turn me from my vocation, simply contenting himself with the statement that I was still very young to make such a serious decision. I defended myself so well that, with Papa's simple and direct character, he was soon convinced my desire was God's will, and in his deep faith he cried out that God was giving him a great honor in asking his children from him (Ms A, 50r°–50v°).

After this tender and moving episode with her dear father Louis, Thérèse believed that she would "be able to fly to Carmel without any fears"; whereas, in reality, "painful trials were still to prove my vocation" (Ms A, 50v°). There's no time to recount them now, but it's useful to recall them, as if

[12] Cf. Gaucher, *Saint Thérèse of Lisieux: The Story of a Life*, 81–82.

in a list: her deputy guardian, Uncle Isidore Guérin, initially refused her entrance into Carmel; Msgr. Delatroëtte, the ecclesiastical superior, refused her entrance as well; the bishop Msgr. Hugonin also postponed his response. Thérèse was resolved to enter, and even took advantage of the diocesan pilgrimage to Rome and the audience with Pope Leo XIII to personally ask the Pope himself to be able to enter into Carmel at fifteen years of age. "If God wills it, you will enter," the Pope responded. Thérèse's determination did not go unobserved, however, in the pilgrimage. Msgr. Révérony, the Vicar General, had changed his mind about Thérèse. At Nice, France, during the return trip, he promised her that he would support her cause.[13] On the eve of Thérèse's fifteenth birthday, that is on January 1st, 1888, she received a letter from the Prioress of Carmel, Mother Marie de Gonzague, bearing good news: Bishop Hugonin had finally given his permission! He had placed the matter in the Prioress's hands, who thankfully supported Thérèse's youthful vocation.

THÉRÈSE'S ENTRANCE INTO THE CARMEL OF LISIEUX AND HER FIRST STEPS IN RELIGIOUS LIFE

And finally, the day so longed for arrived: it was April 9th, 1888, the day of Thérèse's entrance into Carmel! Thérèse soon accustomed herself to the monastery's regulations and way of life. The community was formed at that time by 26 nuns, with an average age of 47. Almost all of them were rather uneducated: at that time schooling usually ended at fifteen years of age. Beside the Prioress and the Martin sisters themselves, only two or three other nuns stood out for education and natural talents.

Although the youngest in the monastery, Thérèse was not deprived of humiliations from various sisters, whereas—contemporarily—she felt need to prevent her own blood sisters, Marie and Pauline, from giving her excessive attention and "motherly" care. She still felt naturally drawn toward the

[13] See ibid., 94–95.

Prioress, and would sometimes hold on tightly to the hand-rail of the stairs when passing near her cell so as to avoid knocking on the Prioress' door in search of some "crumbs" of human consolation.

Although there had been various premonitory signs, the Little Flower—as she is often called—was not expecting a terrible "storm" that was soon to arrive: that is, the sudden aggravation of her beloved father Louis Martin's sickness. On June 23rd, 1888, Louis Martin suddenly disappeared. He was finally found four days later, in a different town, Le Havre, by Céline, Isidore Guérin, and a friend, Ernest Maudelonde. Louis's mind had cleared but he was taken by an obsessive thought: "Withdraw into solitude and live as a hermit." Thérèse could not avoid hearing the tactless remarks and questions of the other nuns in her monastery, as well as the echoes of Lisieux gossip.

Sr. Agnès of Jesus (Pauline), in her compact but precise account of Thérèse's life prepared for the Diocesan Process in 1910, narrated about her little sister:

> On January 11th, 1890, a year and a day after her clothing [ceremony], [Thérèse] was due to make her profession, but Mother Prioress asked her to postpone it; she was afraid that the superior [Msgr. Delatroëtte] would object on the grounds of her youth.
>
> *Asked how the Servant of God reacted to this delay, [Sr. Agnès of Jesus] said:*
>
> I was with the prioress when she informed [Thérèse] of this decision, and I supported this decision myself. Her first reaction was one of disappointment, but almost immediately she understood in prayer that the delay was God's will [...].
>
> She made her profession [Sr. Agnès of Jesus continued] on September 8th, 1890. We could not vote on her admission to the vows without first obtaining the ecclesiastical superior's authorization. He was still rather hesitant, and passed our petition on to the bishop; the latter granted it. Sr. Thérèse's dispositions at the time of her profession are recorded in

> her autobiography, just as she had described them to me. The outstanding features of this period from her entry till she was put in charge of the novices were her humility and her fidelity to the very least of her obligations, despite continual aridity. I know all this from what she used to tell me of her state of soul on the days when the Rule permitted us to talk together.[14]

ST. LOUIS MARTIN'S SICKNESS AND THÉRÈSE'S SPIRITUAL EXPERIENCE

The year that followed Thérèse's Profession and Taking of the Veil ceremony was a year of solitude, of silence, of intimacy with God her Beloved, as well as prayer for sinners and for priests. In the meantime—that is, already before Thérèse's Profession—her beloved father Louis had reached the culmination of his sufferings; on February 12th, 1889, Louis had had an unexpected crisis: fearing battles at Lisieux, he took out his revolver to defend his daughters Léonie and Céline and the maid Maria Cosseron. Uncle Isidore Guérin immediately arranged for Louis's recovery in the psychiatric ward of the *Bon Sauveur* hospital in Caen. Mr. Martin suffered from cerebral arteriosclerosis; he would later be confined to a wheelchair. Thérèse later wrote: "Ah! that day, I didn't say I was able to suffer more! Words cannot express our anguish, and I'm not going to attempt to describe it." In the following month, after her dear father's recovery at the psychiatric ward of *Bon Sauveur*—I wrote about this in my doctoral thesis regarding St. John of the Cross's influence on St. Thérèse—the *petite Thérèse* searched for a light, a guide. She borrowed two books from the library: the *Spiritual Canticle* and the *Living Flame of Love* of St. John of the Cross. With the permission of the Sister Librarian, she was able to keep those two volumes until her death, even on her bedside table in the

[14] Cf. Mother Agnès of Jesus's testimony on Thérèse, in Christopher O'Mahony, ed., *St. Thérèse of Lisieux by Those who Knew Her: Testimonies from the Process of Beatification* (Dublin: Veritas Publications, 2001), 30.

ST. LOUIS MARTIN (THÉRÈSE'S FATHER)

Infirmary during the last months of her life. St. John of the Cross was to become, together with the *Imitation of Christ* and, most especially, the Gospels and St. Paul, a sure guide on Thérèse's spiritual journey.

In the meantime, despite Thérèse's sufferings—or rather, because of her sufferings,—the Spirit of the Lord was strongly at work in Thérèse's soul: her aspirations to love and confidence were strong, but she did not dare to "expand her wings" and take flight in this new way. In her Carmel, as in all of France (and elsewhere) at that time, reigned the pseudo-spirituality of Jansenism. Spiritual fear, scruples, an unhealthy exaggeration of God's punishing Justice, and the idea of a God Who is to be feared and Whom it's better to keep at a certain distance . . . were the order of the day, even in Carmel. One example will suffice: the nuns could receive Communion only with the Prioress's permission! During the annual retreat of 1891, from October 7th–15th, Thérèse was finally set free . . . She had gone to Confession, for the second time during that retreat, with Fr. Alexis Prou, a well-known Franciscan preacher. She would later write: "After speaking only a few words, *I was understood* in a marvelous way and my soul was like a book in which this priest read better than I did myself. He launched me full sail upon the waves of *confidence and love* which so strongly attracted me, but upon which I dared not advance" (Ms A, 80v°).

A NEW "SPRINGTIME" FOR THÉRÈSE

As the long winter of 1891 – 1892 ceased, just so ended another sort of "winter": that of Louis Martin's recovery in the psychiatric ward of the *Bon Sauveur*. After 39 long months Louis was finally dismissed and brought home.[15] Thérèse's soul, as well, began to "thaw out." Nine months later, another decisive event in the Martin family would contribute to a new "springtime" and "blossoming" of this "Little Flower." Mother Marie de Gonzague's term as Prioress was over. On February 20th, 1893, Sr. Agnès of Jesus (Pauline Martin) was elected as the new Prioress. The votes however, had been divided: about half the community were "Pro-Martins," and half "Anti-Martins." Thérèse was fully aware of the delicacy of the situation, and foretold her sister that she would certainly have suffered. Mother Agnès of Jesus chose Thérèse for an extremely delicate task: assist the ex-Prioress Marie de Gonzague, now the novice-mistress, as her "assistant." She would have to be very tactful and wise.

Thérèse, the "Little Flower," slowly blossoming in this new "springtime" of her life, started to express herself not only through painting, but also through other aesthetic means: namely, plays and poems. Now that Sr. Agnès of Jesus was

---

[15] Cf. Gaucher, *Saint Thérèse of Lisieux: The Story of a Life*, 142–43.

Prioress, she no longer had the time to engage in such activities: Thérèse would take her place.[16]

The year after, that is the year 1894, was bound to bring with it some decisive events for Thérèse and the Martin family: first and foremost, the death of their beloved father, Louis Martin. On May 27th Louis suffered an attack of paralysis in his left arm; on June 5th, a heart attack. On July 29th, his holy death, with Céline by his side. Thérèse remained silent, at first... but only to "chant" the first poem that she would write for herself (and not upon request), *Poem* 8, *Prayer of a Child of a Saint.*[17]

THÉRÈSE'S FIRST SYMPTOMS AND HER *WRITINGS*

In the meantime, Thérèse's health also started giving some warning signals: a persistent sore throat, every morning and evening, accompanied by a husky voice. What was the problem? Doctor de Cornière, Mother Marie de Gonzague's trusted physician, proposed some remedies. They were ineffective.[18] Thérèse and her "entourage" slowly realized that she might *not* grow old... One evening during Recreation, a sudden inspiration was destined to mark forever the course of history. Thérèse was amusing her sisters with stories from their childhood. The eldest, Sr. Marie of the Sacred Heart, said to Mother Agnès (Pauline): "Is it possible that you let her write little poems for one or other of the sisters and that she writes nothing about her childhood for us? You will see, she is an angel, she will not stay long on earth, and we will have lost all these details which are so interesting to us." Thérèse laughed. Mother Agnès, instead, turned to her saying: "I order you to write for me all your childhood memories"... Thus was born the text now known as the *Story of a Soul.* Or, rather, the first part of it, called by scholars *Manuscript* A.[19]

---

[16] Cf. ibid., 146–49.
[17] See ibid., 156–57.
[18] See ibid., 159–60.
[19] Cf. ibid., 168.

Thérèse's human and spiritual "blossoming" grew hand in hand with her literary production: as she wrote her childhood memoirs, for obedience, she continued composing poems, plays, and some prayers, as well as keeping up with her letter writing. All was dictated by obedience and charity. Some poems, however, Thérèse wrote spontaneously. Her "masterpiece," or rather the "king" of all of her poetry—as Céline would later define it—is her *Poem 17*: *Vivre d'Amour*: *To Live for Love*. Thérèse composed it during the Forty Hours of Adoration in the choir in preparation for Ash Wednesday, 1895.[20] "Living on Love is giving without limit/ Without claiming wages here below./ Ah! I give without counting, truly sure/ That when one loves, one does not keep count! [...]" (P 17).

THÉRÈSE'S WRITING DESK-DRAWER (WHICH THE CARMELITE NUNS WOULD PLACE ON THEIR LAP) AND HER MANUSCRIPT A

This fruitful year of 1895 would lead to a culmination of Thérèse's spiritual journey, or at least one of its highest peaks: her offering as a victim to God's Merciful Love. During Sunday Mass on June 9th, the Feast of the Holy Trinity, Thérèse received a sudden inspiration: offer herself as a sacrificial victim to God's Merciful Love. Various Carmelite nuns before her time—even Mother Geneviève—had offered themselves

[20] See ibid., 171.

as victims to God's Justice. Thérèse however felt no inclination to do so. She preferred God's Mercy. Or rather: even God's Justice she saw as though illuminated and transfigured by the mystery of God's Mercy. After Mass she dragged her sister Céline (who had entered Carmel in the meantime) over to Mother Agnès (that is, their sister Pauline) to ask her permission. Mother Agnès was distracted by other matters and, completely trusting her sister Thérèse, said that it was fine. Thérèse thus put her offering into writing. Two days later, on June 11th, Thérèse knelt down together with Céline in front of the Statue of Our Lady of Victories and pronounced the offering for herself and on behalf of her sister Céline.[21] This offering was perfectly in line with the "Way" of trust and abandonment to God's Love and Mercy that Fr. Alexis Prou had encouraged her in four years before. Thérèse soon realized that this offering to God's merciful love was not for her alone: besides involving Céline, she soon involved, as well, her sister Marie of the Sacred Heart; then Sr. Marie-Agnès; and then her cousin Marie Guérin, now named Sr. Marie of the Eucharist.[22]

THÉRÈSE'S "PASSION" AND DEATH

Shortly after Mother Marie de Gonzague's re-election as Prioress, on Holy Thursday night—April 3rd, 1896—Thérèse had her first "hemoptysis." She felt "something like a bubbling stream mounting to [her] lips" (Ms C, 4v°). The morning after she brought her pillow to the window: it was as she thought: she had coughed up blood. "*It was like a sweet and distant murmur that announced the Bridegroom's arrival*," she would later write. She told Mother Marie de Gonzague, but not her sister, Sr. Agnès of Jesus. The night after she coughed up blood once more. Her cousin-in-law Dr. Francis La Néele was summoned. He believed that perhaps a blood vessel in her neck had burst, and prescribed some medicines[23]...

---

[21] Cf. ibid., 172–73.
[22] Cf. ibid., 172–75.
[23] See ibid., 186–88.

Thérèse had always imagined that she would die young. Now the "Bridegroom," Jesus, was arriving, although no one had, as of yet, precisely identified her malady. It was tuberculosis . . . Thérèse looked forward to going to Heaven. On Easter Sunday, 1896, however, she experienced—on an interior level—a sudden turn of events. Thérèse would later describe it to Mother Marie de Gonzague: "[God] permitted my soul to be invaded by the thickest darkness, and that the thought of Heaven, up until then so sweet to me, be no longer anything but the cause of struggle and torment" (Ms C, 5v°). It was the night of "*néant*," of nothingness, as Thérèse herself described it (cf. Ms C, 6v°). Thérèse combated these temptations and these "interior voices" by redoubling her acts of faith. "I believe I have made more acts of faith in this past year than all through my whole life" (Ms C, 7r°).

During the summer of the year 1896, Thérèse deeply meditated upon various passages of Isaiah and of St. Paul. The Holy Spirit was "setting the stage," in Thérèse's soul, for a "spectacle" that would turn out to be much more dazzling than her recent Play, *The Triumph of Humility*. In the meantime, on August 6th, Feast of the Transfiguration, Thérèse consecrated herself to the Holy Face, together with the novices Sr. Marie of the Trinity and her sister Céline, called Sr. Geneviève of the Holy Face.[24] It was during her annual private retreat, from the 7th to the 18th of September,[25] however, that the real "spiritual fireworks display" would begin. On September 8th, the six-year anniversary of her final vows, Thérèse wrote a "letter" to Jesus, expressing her gratitude and love. This letter would later become the so-called *Manuscript* B, destined to become one of Thérèse's timeless spiritual masterpieces.

The year 1897—Thérèse's last year here on earth—soon arrived. She was well aware that her time was short. Guy

---

[24] See ibid., 197.

[25] See the "*Chronologie Générale*" ("General Chronology") in G. Gaucher, *Sainte Thérèse de Lisieux (1873–1897). Biographie* (Paris: Les Éditions du Cerf, 2010), in particular 649.

Gaucher, in his book *St. Thérèse of Lisieux: The Story of a Life*, wrote:

> On January 9th, she confided to her little mother (Agnès): "I hope to go there [to Heaven] soon." On the twenty-seventh [of January], to Brother Siméon in Rome, who was eighty-three, she wrote: "I believe that my course here below will not be long." In February, in a letter to Abbé Bellière, she quoted her poem "Vivre d'Amour": "I have the hope that my exile will be short." She added to reassure the seminarian: "If Jesus does what I expect I promise you I will remain your little sister up there."
>
> All that she wrote in these months took on the color of a last will and testament. "My whole soul is there," she said to Mother Agnès when she gave her the poem "My Joy" for her feast day on January 21st.[26]

Besides loving Jesus here on earth, a new desire started to swell up in Thérèse's soul. She had written her eighth play on St. Stanislaus Kostka. She was fascinated by an episode in the saint's life: during a vision of St. Stanislaus, St. Barbara had brought him Holy Communion . . . Could not she, Thérèse, as well, continue to do good on earth even after her death? Could not she, as well, continue to save souls from Heaven?[27]

In the meantime, Thérèse's health, in April and May 1897, deteriorated rapidly. She had various worrying symptoms: digestive troubles, a daily fever "at three o'clock sharp," vomiting, acute chest pains, and most importantly, frequent coughing up of blood. Thérèse slowly had to relinquish all community exercises, such as the Liturgy of the Hours and Recreations, and on May 18th she was exempted from all work duties. During Easter Week, in April, she had spoken quite a bit with Sr. Agnès of Jesus, who started transcribing her words. That little notebook would become the "Yellow Notebook," containing what are known today as Thérèse's *Last Conversations*.

---

[26] Gaucher, *Saint Thérèse of Lisieux: The Story of a Life*, 206–7.

[27] Ibid., 208.

In the month of May, 1897, Thérèse wrote her "Marian testament": her poem *Why I Love You, O Mary!* "There is still one thing I have to do before I die," she confided to Céline. "I have always dreamed of saying in a song to the Blessed Virgin everything I think about her."[28] For Thérèse, Mary is "more Mother than Queen" (CJ 8.21.3).[29] Her 25-verse poem ends with these words:

> Soon I'll go to beautiful Heaven to see you./ You who came *to smile at me* in the morning of my life,/ Come smile at me again . . . Mother. . . . It's evening now!. . . / I no longer fear the splendor of your supreme glory./ With you I've suffered, and now I want/ To sing on your lap, Mary, why I love you,/ And to go on saying that I am your child!. . . . . . (P 54).

At the end of May Thérèse decided to reveal to Sr. Agnès of Jesus (Pauline Martin) that she—Thérèse—had coughed up blood already in 1896. Sr. Agnès was upset. The reality of Thérèse's imminent death hit home. After evening prayer on June 2nd, Sr. Agnès mustered up her courage: she was going to ask Mother Marie de Gonzague to order Thérèse to continue writing her memoirs, before it was too late. She said to Mother Marie de Gonzague,

> Sr. Thérèse wrote for me [. . .] under obedience, some memories of her childhood [. . .]. You would not be able to draw a great deal from them to help you with her [obituary letter] after her death [. . .]. If you commanded her to do it, she could write something more serious, and no doubt you would have something incomparably better than I have.[30]

---

[28] See the commentary to *Poem* 54, *Why I Love You, O Mary!*, in *The Poetry of Saint Thérèse of Lisieux* (Washington D.C.: ICS Publications, 1996), transl. Donald Kinney, O.C.D., 211.

[29] *The Yellow Notebook*, 8.21.3 (August 21st, 1897), in St. Thérèse of Lisieux, *Her Last Conversations* (Washington D.C.: ICS Publications, 1977), transl. John Clarke, O.C.D., 161.

[30] Gaucher, *Saint Thérèse of Lisieux: The Story of a Life*, 218. The quotation is from the Ordinary Process, 146–47. For Sr. Agnès of Jesus's full testimony, in English, see O'Mahony, ed., *St. Thérèse of Lisieux by Those who Knew Her*, 20–73. The quotation above is to be found on page 34.

And so Thérèse began, for obedience, in a small black exercise book, what would later be called her *Manuscript* C. "What should I write about?" Thérèse asked Sr. Agnès. "About the novices, about your spiritual brothers," she replied.[31] Toward the beginning of June, Thérèse said her official farewell to her sisters:

> Oh! little sisters, how happy I am! I see that I'm going to die very soon, I am sure of this now. Don't be astonished if I don't appear to you after my death, and if you see nothing extraordinary as a sign of my happiness. You will remember that it's "my little way" not to desire to see anything [...]. Don't be troubled, little sisters, if I suffer very much and if you see in me, as I've already said, no sign of happiness at the moment of my death. Our Lord really died as a Victim of Love, and you see what His agony was! [...] (CJ 6.4.1).[32]

A month later, on July 8th, Thérèse was transferred to the infirmary. She would remain there until her holy death on September 30th, 1897... Thérèse's last words, while gazing at her crucifix: "Oh! I love Him! ... My God ... I love you! ..." (CJ, September 30th).[33]

---

[31] Cf. Gaucher, *Saint Thérèse of Lisieux: The Story of a Life*, 218.

[32] *The Yellow Notebook*, 6.4.1 (June 4th, 1897), in St. Thérèse of Lisieux, *Her Last Conversations*, transl. Clarke, 55–56.

[33] *The Yellow Notebook*, 30.9 (September 30th, 1897, the day of Thérèse's holy death), in St. Thérèse of Lisieux, *Her Last Conversations*, transl. Clarke, 206–7.

SECOND CHAPTER
St. Thérèse's love for God and for neighbor

INTRODUCTION: THÉRÈSE AND THE GOSPELS

At the end of Thérèse's *Manuscript* A—on the third to the last page, to be precise—Thérèse mentions her love for the Gospels. She wrote,

> If I open a book composed by a spiritual author [...], I feel my heart contract immediately and I read without understanding, so to speak. Or if I do understand, my mind comes to a standstill without the capacity of meditating. In this helplessness, Holy Scripture and the *Imitation* come to my aid; in them I discover a solid and very *pure* nourishment. But it is especially the *Gospels* that sustain me during my hours of prayer, for in them I find what is necessary for my poor little soul. I am constantly discovering in them new lights, hidden and mysterious meanings (Ms A, 83r°–83v°).

Thérèse herself, in this passage, testifies to the fact that she assiduously meditated the Gospels. This should not be too surprising, considering that the central precept of the original Carmelite rule—which the Lisieux Carmelites lived by, and read in its entirety every Friday, during the meal;—as I was saying, the central precept of St. Albert of Jerusalem's Rule was that of "meditating, day and night, the Lord's law."

THÉRÈSE, THE CARMEL OF LISIEUX, AND THE SACRED SCRIPTURES

Nonetheless, in Thérèse's time—even among cloistered and even Carmelite nuns,—frequent personal meditation of the Gospels was not a common practice. As a matter of fact, the Bible in general was hard to find in cloistered monasteries, at least in *female* cloistered monasteries. The pseudo-spirituality of Jansenism, which poisoned the spiritual climate of Thérèse's time, also censured those books of the Bible which were considered to be indecent, especially *The Song of Songs*, but—in reality—the Old Testament in general.[1] Thérèse, instead, turned almost instinctively to God's Word, contained in the Holy Scriptures, for light and guidance on her spiritual journey. The Martin family had two copies of the entire Bible—Old and New Testament—but it seems that Thérèse did *not* study them before entering Carmel. She did, however, benefit from the daily readings, in the Martin homestead, of Dom Guéranger's multiple-volume *Année liturgique*, a commentary on the Biblical readings of the Liturgical Year. She also listened attentively, of course, to the priests' homilies during Sunday Mass, who commented and explained that Sunday's Readings. And, whenever Thérèse gleaned some passage of the Scriptures in one of her personal readings, as a teenager, she would immediately entrust it to her prodigious memory. We must remember that Thérèse had memorized *The Imitation of Christ*, as a child and young teenager, practically by heart (which, by the way, is full of quotations of the Scriptures). Once Thérèse entered Carmel, she drew abundantly from the Psalms in the Liturgy of the Hours. She did not understand Latin—true enough—however there was an integral translation of the Psaltery in French, available in the Carmel. And sometimes, during her conversations or her lessons for the novices, she would quote the Psalms in Latin, and comment them. So, through intuition and a bit of seeking around, Thérèse could find out the sense of the passages that seemed most interesting to her. Most importantly, Thérèse asked Céline—while still in the world—to have a copy of the Gospels (two copies, actually) custom-made and bound for her, in an especially small format. She wanted to carry them upon her heart, like St. Cecilia, one of the saints whom Thérèse loved most, who, according to the legend, carried the Gospels upon her heart. And so Thérèse did . . . And soon

[1] For this section of my study, I will be borrowing various concepts from Guy Gaucher's excellent *Introduction* to the book *La Bible avec Thérèse de Lisieux*, Sr. Cécile, of the Carmel de Lisieux, and Sr. Geneviève, O.P., of the Monastery of Clairefontaine, eds. (Paris: Les Éditions du Cerf, 1990), 9–41.

her novices and other nuns in the Lisieux Carmel imitated her. Thérèse would often pull out her little copy of the Gospels and read it and meditate upon it. She would also later benefit from a small black notebook that Céline would bring with her when entering Carmel, with various passages of the Old Testament. Thérèse borrowed Céline's black notebook for a year-and-a-half's time. The novices that Thérèse led and gave lessons to would later testify that Thérèse's lessons consisted practically in a spontaneous explanation and comment on the Sacred Scriptures. In fact, Thérèse quotes the Bible more than one thousand times in her writings: about 440 quotations from the Old Testament and 650 from the New Testament. Her writings are full of the Sacred Scriptures, which Thérèse would draw (and quote), in most cases, directly from her memory in the little time she had to compose her Poetry, her Plays, or her Letters or Autobiography.

THE GOSPELS: THÉRÈSE'S MAIN SOURCE OF INSPIRATION FOR HER EXPERIENCE OF "FRATERNAL CHARITY"

Now, you may be asking yourself: why speak so much about Thérèse's love for the Gospels? I've spoken about Thérèse's love for the Sacred Scriptures, and most especially for the Gospels, because it is precisely the Gospels which became Thérèse's main source of inspiration and which she was able to read in a "fresh" way and re-propose to modern-day society. This is true of all of Thérèse's spirituality—especially her "Little Way"—and is equally true as regards her experience and doctrine about fraternal charity.

Jesus Himself summarized the entirety of the Law in His genius, two-fold commandment: love God and love your neighbor. Let's take a quick glance at the Gospels to refresh our memory. In all three of the Synoptics—Matthew, Mark, and Luke—Jesus responds to the expert in the law, who had questioned Him about which was the greatest of the commandments, with a two-fold quotation: Jesus quotes Deuteronomy 6:5 and Leviticus 19:18. That is: "Love the Lord your

God with all your heart and with all your soul and with all your strength" (Dt 6:5), and "Love your neighbor as yourself" (Lev 19:18). (The novelty here, in Jesus's teaching, is not the ideas or the laws in themselves, but rather the choice of these two passages, and their molding into one.) According to Matthew's Gospel, Jesus then adds: "All the Law and the Prophets hang on these two commandments" (cf. Mt 22:34–40). Whereas, in Mark, Jesus comments: "There is no commandment greater than these" (see Mk 12:28–34). In Luke, on the other hand, the expert in the law insists by asking Jesus: "Who is my neighbor?" And Jesus responds by recounting the parable of the Good Samaritan. He concludes by addressing the expert in the law and challenging him, saying: "Go and do likewise" (cf. Lk 10:25–37).

THÉRÈSE'S INTERPRETATION OF THE GOSPELS CONCERNING FRATERNAL CHARITY

Most certainly Thérèse knew these passages of the Gospels. Actually, she quotes them while speaking of fraternal charity. Thérèse wrote:

> This year, dear Mother, God has given me the grace to understand what charity is; I understood it before, it is true, but in an imperfect way. I had never fathomed the meaning of these words of Jesus: *"The second commandment is* LIKE *the first: You shall love your neighbor as yourself."* I applied myself especially to loving God, and it is in loving Him that I understood my love was not to be expressed only in words, for: *"It is not those who say: 'Lord, Lord!' who will enter the kingdom of heaven, but those who do the will of my Father in heaven"* (Ms C, 11v°).

Here Thérèse quotes, specifically, the Gospel of Matthew, chapter 22, verse 39, which we have already seen together just now. Her interpretation, however, is interesting and quite unique. First of all, she herself underlines, with her pen, and thus accentuates, the word LIKE (*semblable*). Thérèse thus recognizes, in Jesus's two-fold commandment, a sort of equality or intimate connection between charity toward God and toward neighbor that she had never realized before. In fact, in the next line, she admits: "I applied myself especially to loving God." Yet—here is Thérèse's discovery—it was precisely through living the experience of a strong love for God that she found the necessity to love her neighbor. She wrote: "I applied myself especially to loving God, and it is in loving Him that I understood my love was not to be expressed only in words." Thérèse then explains herself more clearly, in the following lines:

> Jesus has revealed this will [of His Father in Heaven] several times or I should say on almost every page of His Gospel. But at the Last Supper, when He knew the hearts of His disciples were burning with a more ardent love for Him Who had just given Himself to them in the unspeakable mystery of His Eucharist, this sweet Savior wished to give them a *new commandment*. He said to them with inexpressible tenderness: *"A new commandment I give you that you love one another: THAT AS I HAVE LOVED YOU, YOU ALSO LOVE ONE ANOTHER. By this will all men know that you are my disciples, if you have love for one another"* (Ms C, 11v°).

While quoting Jesus's New Commandment on the reciprocal love that His disciples must have for one another, "That as I have loved you, you also love one another," Thérèse puts these words into italics, and underlines them various times. It is precisely Jesus's New Commandment, given in the Last Supper, which inspires and motivates Thérèse's discovery and experience of fraternal charity.

It's interesting to see how Thérèse interprets and comments this Gospel passage. She wrote: "How did Jesus love His disciples and why did He love them? Ah! it was not their natural qualities that could have attracted Him, since there was between Him and them an infinite distance" (Ms C, 12r°). Thérèse was all too aware of what it meant to love other people who had no or very few natural qualities. Perhaps you've already had the opportunity to see some photographs of

Thérèse's monastic community,[2] and it must be remembered that—besides the Martin clan—only two or three other nuns in the Lisieux Carmel had a good education. Only a few pages after these lines on Jesus's New Commandment, Thérèse refers to a sister whom she found particularly difficult to love, as an example of how to live Jesus's New Commandment. She wrote: "There is in the community a sister who has the talent of displeasing me in everything, in her ways, her words, her character, everything seems *very disagreeable* [underlined] to me" (Ms C, 13v°). How, then, does Thérèse learn to love this sister? She continues: "And still, she is a holy religious who must be very pleasing to God. Not wishing to give in to the natural antipathy that I was experiencing, I told myself that charity must not consist in feelings but in works" (ibid.). Thérèse teaches at least three very important truths in this passage: first of all, that only God can judge our hearts. "She [...] must be very pleasing to God." Secondly, that a positive attitude is always the best: as the optimists would say, "The glass is half full." Thérèse, in fact, states: "She is a holy religious." So, not being able to judge her sister's heart and the level of her charity, Thérèse gives her the benefit of the doubt: "She is a holy religious." Lastly, Thérèse reminds us that charity is not a question of feelings. It's a question of works. She continues, writing:

> Then I set myself to doing for this sister what I would do for the person I loved the most. Each time I met her I prayed to God for her, offering Him all her virtues and merits. I felt this was pleasing to Jesus, for there is no artist who doesn't love to receive praise for his works, and Jesus, the artist of souls, is happy when we don't stop at the exterior, but, penetrating into the inner sanctuary where He chooses to dwell, we admire its beauty. I wasn't content simply with praying very much for this sister who gave me so many struggles, but I took care to render her all the services possible,

---

[2] I have provided 6 photos of Thérèse's fellow nuns in this book. See the cover and also: *infra*, pp. 27, 35, 41, 91, 121, 125.

> and when I was tempted to answer her back in a disagreeable manner, I was content with giving her my most friendly smile, and with changing the subject of the conversation (Ms C, 13v°–14r°).

SR. THÉRÈSE OF ST. AUGUSTIN: A WITNESS TO THÉRÈSE'S FRATERNAL CHARITY

The nun whom Thérèse is referring to, who had "a talent of displeasing [her] in everything," was Sr. Thérèse of St. Augustin. This nun actually never found out, nor ever imagined, that the nun Thérèse described was actually her very self![3] Sr. Thérèse of St. Augustin would later write, in her *Preparatory Notes for the Apostolic Process* of Thérèse's canonization, the following words:

> In community life, the Servant of God practiced the most exquisite charity, constantly forgetting herself for the happiness of the sisters, enduring without complaint and without anyone noticing the suffering caused to her by the malice and jealousy of some sisters who failed to recognize her virtue, always remaining patient, gentle, and kind with them, welcoming them with a gracious smile, avoiding anything that might upset them, trying to be pleasant to them and constantly excusing them. When she met a sister for whom her nature was a little distant, she prayed for her and offered to God the virtues she had noticed in her [...].
>
> She was ingenious at finding ways to show compassion to the sisters she knew to be suffering or afflicted. With ravishing delicacy, she would say a word, or just smile if she couldn't do more. But this sympathy went straight to the heart, you knew it was genuine, and an atmosphere of peace reigned around her; you felt you were close to an angel![4]

[3] Cf. Ste. Thérèse de l'énfant Jesus et de la Sainte-Face, *Manuscrits autobiographiques*, "Nouvelle Édition du Centenaire," [*Nouvelle édition revue et corrigée*] (Lonrai: Éditions du Cerf, Desclée de Brouwer, 2005), 360 (footnote regarding *Manuscript* C, 13v°, 18).

[4] https://archives.carmeldelisieux.fr/en/au-carmel-du-temps-de-therese/la-communaute/soeur-therese-de-st-augustin/notes-preparatoires-de-sr-therese-de-st-augustin/ (accessed on April 1st, 2025).

SR. THÉRÈSE OF ST. AUGUSTIN

These words of Sr. Thérèse of St. Augustin, who is precisely that nun whom Thérèse found the most difficulty loving, are the proof that Thérèse had not only understood the meaning of Jesus's New Commandment, but that she also lived it fully! Thérèse, in fact, wrote in *Manuscript* C: "When Jesus gave His apostles a new commandment, HIS OWN COMMANDMENT, as He calls it later on, it is no longer a question of loving one's neighbor as oneself but of loving him as *He, Jesus, has loved him*, and will love him to the consummation of the ages" (Ms C, 12v°). It's important to realize, though, that Thérèse was able to live out Jesus's New Commandment to its fullness precisely because of her "Little Way." She did not base her charity on her own strength, but on God's grace. The next lines, in fact, read as follows:

> Ah! Lord, I know You don't command the impossible. You know better than I do my weakness and imperfection; You know very well that never would I be able to love my sisters as You love them, unless *You*, O my Jesus, *loved them in me*. It is because You wanted to give me this grace that You made Your new commandment. Oh! how I love this new commandment since it

> gives me the assurance that your Will is *to love in me* all those you command me to Love! (Ms C, 12v°)

Thérèse realizes that, if she is able to love her sisters with genuine charity, it is because it is Jesus Himself who is loving them in her. The next line is: "Yes, I feel it, when I am charitable, it is Jesus alone who is acting in me, and the more united I am to Him, the more also do I love my sisters" (ibid.).

CONCLUSIVE THOUGHTS

Reassuming what has been said so far concerning Thérèse's charity for God and for neighbor, and the unbreakable tie between the two loves, which Jesus Himself established, I would say the following: Thérèse's love for the Sacred Scriptures lead her—in the light of the Holy Spirit—to penetrate and understand their true meaning; this is especially true for the Gospels. Thérèse was able to go straight to the "heart of the matter," and underline the most important passages of the Gospel, the most essential ones. Jesus's two-fold commandment on love for God and for neighbor, and especially Jesus's New Commandment, are certainly two of the most important passages in the Gospels; and it is precisely on those two evangelical passages that Thérèse builds the theological foundation for her experience of fraternal charity.

THIRD CHAPTER
St. Thérèse's charity toward her family members

INTRODUCTION:
FRATERNAL CHARITY IN THE MARTIN FAMILY

When approaching the subject of this chapter—St. Thérèse's charity toward her family members—it's important to remember that not only has Thérèse been canonized, but also both of her parents, Louis and Zélie Martin, have been canonized. Léonie Martin's process of canonization is also well on the way. Therefore, it's logical to assume—and so it was—that in the Martin family, charity was an everyday reality. Thérèse grew up in a charitable atmosphere, where natural and supernatural charity were regularly practiced—at least by her parents—even on a heroic level, as will be the case for Thérèse herself. It is in and from this spiritually fertile "terrain," so to speak, that the "Little Flower," Thérèse, will grow, develop, and blossom.

THÉRÈSE'S INFANCY AND SISTERS

Let's take a closer look at her household environment, while growing up. Thérèse would later write:

> God was pleased all through my life to surround me with *love*, and the first memories I have are stamped with smiles and the most tender caresses. But although He placed so much *love* near me, He also sent much love into my little heart, making it warm and affectionate. I loved Mama and Papa very much and showed my tenderness for them in a thousand ways, for I was very expressive (Ms A, 4v°).

Thérèse mentions in this passage that her first memories were "stamped with smiles and the most tender caresses." We can assume that Thérèse is referring here not only to her dear parents, but also to her four sisters: Marie, Pauline, Léonie, and Céline. In fact, Thérèse had a special relationship with each one of her sisters, as well. Recalling her childhood memories, Thérèse wrote:

> I was very fond of my *godmother* [Marie]. Without appearing to do so, I paid close attention to what was said and done around me. It seems to me that I was judging things then as I do now. I was listening carefully to what Marie was teaching Céline in order to do what Céline did (ibid.).

Here Thérèse tells of her fondness for Marie, but also of her close attention to Marie and to her "teachings" to Céline. However, Thérèse felt inclined not only to imitate her eldest sister, Marie, but even to imitate her youngest older sister, Céline, not even four years older than her! Thérèse continued shortly after:

> Dear little Léonie held a warm place in my heart. She was very fond of me and in the evenings when the family took a walk she used to take care of me. I still seem to hear those beautiful lullabies she used to sing to me to get me to sleep. She was always trying to find ways of pleasing me, and I would be sorry if I caused her any trouble (Ms A, 6r°).

Léonie was sort of the "black sheep" of the Martin family, in the sense that she had a particular temperament and way of being. She was also the one who struggled the most to find her religious vocation. Léonie tried the Poor Clares, but did not find her way there; she later entered, exited, and then re-entered the Visitandines in Caen, where she would then remain for the rest of her life. However, paradoxically, it seems that Léonie was the one—among Thérèse's siblings—who most deeply understood and practiced Thérèse's "Little Way." Perhaps having had a "late start," with less natural talents than the others, grounded Léonie in that humility and littleness that was necessary to better understand Thérèse's heart and her "Little Way."

Thérèse wrote, again in the first pages of her *Manuscript* A:

THE MARTIN SISTERS, FROM ELDEST TO YOUNGEST: MARIE (TOP LEFT), PAULINE (TOP RIGHT), LÉONIE (BOTTOM LEFT), CÉLINE (BOTTOM RIGHT, ON THE LEFT), AND THÉRÈSE (BOTTOM RIGHT, ON THE RIGHT)

> I was very proud of my two sisters [Marie and Céline], but the one who was my *ideal* from childhood was Pauline. When I was beginning to talk, Mama would ask me: "What are you thinking about?" and I would answer invariably: "Pauline!" (Ms A, 6v°).

St. Thérèse's thought, as a toddler, was continuously directed toward her "ideal," Pauline. This experience, perhaps funny in some ways, also proved to be providential. Thérèse wrote, two lines after:

> I had often heard it said that surely Pauline would become a *religious*, and without knowing too much

> about what it meant I thought: "I too *will be a religious.*" This is one of my first memories and I haven't changed my resolution since then! It was through you, dear Mother, that Jesus chose to espouse me to Himself [...]. You were my *ideal*; I wanted to be like you, and it was your example that drew me toward the Spouse of Virgins at the age of two (Ms A, 6r°).

As Thérèse herself wrote in these few lines, her sister Pauline was influential, or rather vital, in God's providential plan for Thérèse. Thérèse, two years later, that is, at the age of four, would choose Pauline as her "second mother," at her mother Zélie's funeral, imitating Céline who chose the eldest sister Marie as her "second mother."

THÉRÈSE AND HER MOTHER ZÉLIE

As far as Thérèse's love toward her mother Zélie is concerned, one example will suffice. (We've already spoken briefly of their special rapport in our first chapter, on Thérèse's biographical experience.) In a letter that Zélie wrote to Pauline on February 13th, 1877, Zélie recounted to her second-born a touching episode concerning Thérèse:

> The other day I wanted to kiss Thérèse before going downstairs. She seemed to be in a deep sleep, and I didn't dare wake her up when Marie said to me, "Mama, she's pretending to be asleep, I'm sure of it." Then, I bent down over her forehead to kiss her, but she immediately hid herself under the blanket, saying to me, sounding like a spoiled child, "I don't want anyone to look at me." I was less than pleased, and I let her know it. Two minutes later I heard her crying, and the next thing I knew, to my great surprise, I saw her at my side! She'd left her little bed all by herself and came down the stairs barefoot, encumbered by her nightgown which was longer than she was. Her little face was covered in tears. "Mama," she said, while throwing herself at my knees, "I was naughty, forgive me!" Forgiveness was quickly given. I took my little angel in my arms, pressing her to my heart and covering her with kisses.

> When she saw herself so well received, she said to me, "Oh! Mama, if only you wanted to wrap me in a blanket like when I was little! I'd eat my chocolate here at the table." I took the trouble to go look for her blanket and then I wrapped her in it like when she was little. I looked like I was playing with a doll![1]

Moments with her dear mother Zélie, so precious and tender like these, would unfortunately soon come to an end for Thérèse. Only six months after this moving episode, her mother Zélie passed away.

THÉRÈSE AND HER FATHER LOUIS

As I mentioned in our first chapter, Thérèse's father Louis had a special affection and love toward Thérèse, as did she for him. Thérèse wrote:

> I must admit, Mother, my happy disposition completely changed after Mama's death. I, once so full of life, became timid and retiring, sensitive to an excessive degree [...]. I could not bear the company of strangers and found my joy only within the intimacy of the family.
>
> And still I continued to be surrounded with the most delicate *tenderness*. Our father's *very affectionate* heart seemed to be enriched now with a truly maternal love! You and Marie, Mother, were you not *the most tender* and selfless of mothers? Ah! if God had not showered His beneficent rays upon His little flower, she could never have accustomed herself to earth, for she was too weak to stand up against the rains and the storms. She needed warmth, a gentle dew, and the springtime breezes. Never were these lacking. Jesus had her find them beneath the snow of trial! (Ms A, 13r°–13v°).

Thérèse readily admits her weaknesses: "She [Thérèse]

---

[1] See the Archives of the Carmel of Lisieux website, under the tab "Family Environment—Correspondence"; "Filter by senders—Zélie Guérin," on the date February 13th, 1877: https://archives.carmeldelisieux.fr/en/correspondance/de-mme-martin-a-pauline-cf-188-13-fevrier-1877/ (accessed on April 1st, 2025).

was too weak to stand up against the rains and the storms" of this earth. Yet, she realizes God's protective intervention on her behalf: "She needed warmth, a gentle dew [...]. Jesus had her find them beneath the snow of trial!" The affection and motherly love of her two eldest sisters, and even of her father Louis—whose heart, after Zélie's death, "seemed to be enriched now with a truly maternal love!"—at least partially substituted her mother Zélie's absence. Only the Blessed Virgin Mary, Mother of God and Mother of the Church, would finally and fully heal Thérèse's mourning heart, after the loss of her mother Zélie; it was Her "ravishing smile," on Pentecost Sunday, 1883, which instantaneously healed Thérèse of that "strange sickness" that no one was able to diagnosticate. (On that day, Thérèse discovered in the Blessed Virgin Mary a true "second mother," to not say a "first Mother," and her relationship with Mary grew from then on.)

THÉRÈSE'S UNCLE ISIDORE GUÉRIN AND AUNT CÉLINE FOURNET, AND HER COUSINS JEANNE AND MARIE GUÉRIN

Another family relation worthy of mentioning is that of Thérèse with her dear Aunt and Uncle, and cousins. Zélie's brother, Isidore Guérin, had invited Louis to come to Lisieux together with his five daughters, to be closer to the family. Every Sunday, in fact, the Martins and the Guérins would spend the evening together. Thérèse would also walk back and forth from school at the Benedictine Abbey together with her two cousins, Marie and Jeanne Guérin, whom Thérèse loved dearly; they would also go on summer vacations together.

I could continue about Thérèse's ties of affection and love for her family members, but I feel that this essential sort of "sketch" is enough, as regards Thérèse's life before entering Carmel. What is more important, I believe, is to see how Thérèse lived her family ties, and charity toward her family members after her entrance into Carmel.

LEFT: MR. ISIDORE GUÉRIN AND MRS. CÉLINE FOURNET.

RIGHT: JEANNE (LEFT) AND MARIE (RIGHT) GUÉRIN. JEANNE LATER MARRIED DR. FRANCIS LA NÉELE; MARIE LATER JOINED THE LISIEUX CARMEL (SR. MARIE OF THE EUCHARIST) AND BECAME THÉRÈSE'S NOVICE.

WHAT DROVE THÉRÈSE TO ENTER CARMEL?

Thérèse herself describes the reason why she entered Carmel: "I had declared at the feet of Jesus-Victim, in the examination preceding my profession, what I had come to Carmel for: 'I came to save souls and especially to pray for priests'" (Ms A, 69v°). Now, I'm quoting this for a reason: note that Thérèse did not respond: "I came to follow my elder sisters, who took the place of my mother for me, after her death"; or, "I came to follow and to find my sisters, who preceded me in Carmel."

Thérèse, in fact, did not enter Carmel to be together with her family members. Her motivations were much more profound and much more all-embracing than that. And this is what drove Thérèse to transform her previous family ties from a simple tie of affection and love to a tie of supernatural charity.

THÉRÈSE'S FRATERNAL CHARITY TOWARD HER FAMILY MEMBERS DURING HER YEARS AS A CARMELITE

We must now examine more closely Thérèse's charity toward her family members after her entrance into Carmel. The day before and of her entrance—April 9th, 1888—were certainly not easy for Thérèse. She wrote in *Manuscript* A:

> The evening before [my entrance], the whole family gathered round the table where I was to sit for the last time. Ah! how heartrending these family reunions can really be! When you would like to see yourself forgotten, the most tender caresses and words are showered upon you, making the sacrifice of separation felt all the more (Ms A, 68v°).

Even harder, for Thérèse, was the day after, the day of her entrance into Carmel. She continued:

> As on the evening before, the whole family was reunited to hear Holy Mass and receive Communion. As soon as Jesus descended into the hearts of my relatives, I heard nothing around me but sobs. I was the only one who didn't shed any tears, but my heart was beating *so violently* it seemed impossible to walk when they signaled for me to come to the enclosure door [...]. After embracing all the members of the family, I knelt down before my matchless father for his blessing, and to give it to me he placed *himself on his knees* and blessed me, tears flowing down his cheeks [...]. A few moments later, the doors of the holy ark closed upon me (Ms A, 69r°).

Thérèse had crossed the threshold of Carmel! Never again would she exit from its doors. She was now called to live an *interior* journey, a journey of love—toward God and toward her neighbor. Let's see how, in particular toward her own family members, for now. It's worth mentioning that, crossing Carmel's threshold, Thérèse felt—notwithstanding the "sacrifice of separation" from her dear father and from her family—a deep peace. She wrote: "My desires were at last accomplished; my soul experienced a PEACE so sweet, so deep, it would be impossible to express it. For seven and a half years that inner peace has remained my lot, and has not abandoned me in the midst of the greatest trials" (Ms A, 69r°–69v°).

THÉRÈSE'S CORRESPONDENCE WITH HER FATHER LOUIS

Thérèse's first letters, in fact, have a happy and carefree tone. The first letter that she wrote, from Carmel, was addressed to her dear father Louis. April 28th—twenty days after Thérèse's entrance—was Céline's nineteenth birthday. They celebrated it in the parlor of the Lisieux Carmel. Louis Martin however, was not able to attend the birthday party, so Thérèse, the following day, sent him a letter. She often effused her thanksgivings in her letters to her dear father Louis, who truly was very generous. Almost every day he would leave a present for the Carmel of Lisieux in the turn or "wheel" of the monastery.[2] Most often it was food. The Carmel of Lisieux, in fact, was poor. Thérèse wrote:

> Dear little Father,
>
> How good you are, then, to your little Queen; almost no day passes that she does not receive some present from her King.
>
> Thanks for everything, good little Father. If you only knew how much the little *Orpheline de la Bérésina* loves you! But, no, you will know this only in Heaven [...].
>
> Dear little Father, I see the hour is going by, and I must leave you, but beforehand I kiss you from a distance with my whole heart (LT 46).

Thérèse was always particularly affectionate and thankful to her dear and saintly father, Louis Martin. She also was, really, toward all of her family members, both outside and inside of Carmel.

---

[2] See the Introduction to the Postulancy Period of Thérèse's *Letters* in St. Thérèse of the Child Jesus and of the Holy Face, *Letters of St. Thérèse of Lisieux: General Correspondence*, vol. 1 (1877–1890), ed. J. Clarke (Washington, D.C.: ICS Publications, 1982), 413–20.

INTERIOR STRUGGLES AND THE PURIFICATION OF THÉRÈSE'S NATURAL AFFECTION

When Thérèse entered, her two eldest sisters, Marie and Pauline, had already been attending her, having entered some years before. Thérèse's affection for her sisters in Carmel, however, immediately assumed a spiritual and supernatural tone. Thérèse would often write to her sister Pauline—her "second mother"—who also became, in a certain sense, a spiritual guide for Thérèse, together with her spiritual director (soon to be quite absent), Fr. Pichon, and of course the Prioress, Mother Marie de Gonzague (a very peculiar character). On July 4th, 1888, a few months after her entrance to Carmel, Thérèse wrote to Sr. Agnes of Jesus (that is, Pauline): "The bleating of Jesus's dear lamb has resounded like sweet music in the ears of the little lamb." (Thérèse plays on the fact that Pauline had taken the religious name of Agnes—from the Latin *Agnus*, meaning "Lamb"—whose iconography often depicts her as carrying a lamb, also sign of the virgin and martyr's innocence. "Jesus's dear lamb" is Pauline; the "little lamb" is Thérèse.) She continued: "Jesus alone! Nothing but Him. The grain of sand is so little that, if it wanted to place someone other than Him in its heart, there would be no room for Jesus" (LT 54). The editor comments in footnote: "This is a probable reference to her very deep affection for Mother Marie de Gonzague."[3]

At this point, I think it could be useful to reflect on Thérèse's natural inclination to use affection toward others, and how she was able to channel that affection toward Jesus—in the first place—and toward her neighbor, but in an ordinate fashion, which allowed her to avoid any harmful or morbid attachments. In her *Manuscript* C, written of course in June 1897, therefore only a few months before her death, Thérèse reminisces and explains how she was able to do so. She addressed her *Manuscript* C to Mother Marie de Gonzague. Thérèse wrote:

[3] St. Thérèse, *Letters of St. Thérèse of Lisieux: General Correspondence*, vol. 1, 441.

> I remember when I was still a postulant that I had such violent temptations to satisfy myself and to find a few crumbs of pleasure that I was obliged to walk rapidly by your door and to cling firmly to the banister of the staircase in order not to turn back. There came into my mind a crowd of permissions to seek; in a word, dear Mother, I found a thousand reasons for pleasing my nature. How happy I am now for having deprived myself from the very beginning of my religious life! I no longer feel the necessity of refusing all human consolations, for my soul is strengthened by Him whom I wanted to love uniquely. I can see with joy that in loving Him the heart expands and can give to those who are dear to it incomparably more tenderness than if it had concentrated upon one egotistical and unfruitful love (Ms C, 21v°–22r°).

We must remember that Thérèse was very fond of Mother Marie de Gonzague, especially during the first months of her religious life, before discovering her grievous faults. After all, Thérèse had met her and looked up to her since she was only nine years old. They also kept up correspondence by letter and through Sr. Agnes, that is, Pauline. It was Mother Marie de Gonzague who had vouched to the bishop for Thérèse's maturity and obtained permission for her entrance into Carmel. However, Thérèse was able to check and temper this natural affection toward Mother Marie de Gonzague through exertion and courage. It's important, again, to recall Thérèse's naturally affectionate character. She wrote:

> My heart, sensitive and affectionate as it was, would have easily surrendered had it found a heart capable of understanding it [...]. When I noticed Céline showing affection for one of her teachers, I wanted to imitate her, but not *knowing* how to win the good grace of creatures, I was unable to succeed. O blessed ignorance! which has helped me avoid great evils! How can I thank Jesus for making me find *"only bitterness in earth's friendships"*! With a heart such as mine, I would have allowed myself to be taken and my wings to be clipped, and then how would I have been able

> to *"fly and be at rest"*? How can a heart given over to the affection of creatures be intimately united with God? I feel this is not possible. Without having drunk the poisoned cup of a too ardent love of creatures, I *feel* I cannot be mistaken. I have seen so many souls, seduced by this *false light*, fly like poor moths and burn their wings, and then return to the real and gentle light of *Love* that gives them new wings which are more brilliant and delicate, so that they can fly toward Jesus, that Divine Fire "which burns without consuming" [...].
>
> I know that without Him, I could have fallen as low as St. Mary Magdalene [...], but I also know that Jesus *has forgiven me more* than *St. Mary Magdalene* since He forgave me *in advance* by preventing me from falling (Ms A, 38r°-38v°).

A STRIKING DIFFERENCE: THÉRÈSE COMPARED WITH HER SISTERS PAULINE AND MARIE

In this important passage—a bit long, perhaps,—Thérèse expresses the nature of her "sensitive and affectionate" heart; and, furthermore, how Jesus preserved her from attaching herself in a disordinate way to any "creature," that is, human person. Could her expression "I have seen so many souls, seduced by this *false light*" be referring even to her own sisters, Pauline and Marie? In fact, it seems that neither Pauline nor Marie shared Thérèse's courage and self-denial... Both of them did not check themselves in indulging in useless and self-satisfying conversations with the Mother Prioress. Although Mother Marie de Gonzague had a peculiar character, she also had many qualities: a beautiful voice, a charming charisma, intelligence, and culture. Pauline and Marie, deprived at a young age of their natural mother, probably found comfort and human satisfaction in Mother Marie de Gonzague, but unfortunately in a disordinate fashion. Sr. Agnes of Jesus (Pauline Martin) wrote a note to her sister Marie of the Sacred Heart (Marie Martin) in May of 1888, that is, in the same time period when Thérèse herself was struggling to check her natural affection toward Mother Marie de Gonzague; Pauline wrote:

MOTHER MARIE DE GONZAGUE (PRIORESS OF THE LISIEUX CARMEL)

> I will not see our Mother [Marie de Gonzague] until tomorrow, I think. Just recently I suffered a little because I gave in to the desire of seeing her today. This will be three days; that is long. But how blind we are; who will deliver us from our darkness? To be always wanting to satisfy ourselves, always enjoying something![4]

As you can tell, the tone of Pauline's note to her elder sister Marie is entirely different than that of Thérèse's note, marked by her struggle to overcome her natural inclinations, but also by peace and spiritual well-being. Marie expressed herself,

---

[4] See the footnote 2 of *LC* 80 in St. Thérèse, *Letters of St. Thérèse of Lisieux: General Correspondence*, vol. 1, 426.

years later, in her Preparatory Notes for the Ordinary Process of Thérèse's beatification, along the same lines as her sister Pauline. She wrote:

> One day, [Thérèse and I] were passing our Mother [Marie de Gonzague's] cell together, and I made a sign to her to come in with me. But instead of following me, she quickly descended the stairs to distract herself from the temptation of seeking herself in anything. Seeing her heroism, I admit that I was embarrassed when I compared myself to her.[5]

This testimony of Marie, Thérèse's eldest sister, not only portrays her (unfortunate) lack of virtue; it also manifests Thérèse's heroic virtue and the supernatural character of her love, or charity.

THE PURITY OF THÉRÈSE'S LOVE

Considering Thérèse's way of conquering her natural but disordinate affection for Mother Marie de Gonzague sheds a great light on how Thérèse did the same toward her sisters, in Carmel. The precedent testimonies also show, by contrast, that Pauline and Marie did not exercise the same virtue in their way of relating with Thérèse, which of course made things all the more difficult for Thérèse and allowed her to temper her virtues all the more. It's extremely enlightening to hear some passages of Marie Martin's testimony on her sister Thérèse, regarding her supernatural and fraternal charity. Marie wrote:

> [Thérèse's] fortitude manifested itself too in her relations with a certain sister for whom she felt a great aversion. She hid her aversion so well that I thought she loved this sister very much, and I felt jealous. One day I said to her: "I cannot help telling you in confidence about something that is annoying me . . . I think you love Sister—more than me, and I don't think it's fair. After all, God made family ties. You always seem so pleased to see her that I cannot think otherwise,

[5] Cf. ibid.

> since you have never shown such happiness about being with me." [Thérèse] laughed heartily at this, but she gave me no idea of the aversion she felt for this religious.[6]

Marie speaks of Thérèse's fraternal charity toward her nun sisters, and her way of checking her natural affection and inclination toward her (blood) sisters in another occasion, in her Preparatory Notes for the Ordinary Process of Thérèse's beatification, written in 1908, that is, eleven years after Thérèse's death. Marie wrote:

> From the very first days of her novitiate, I saw the degree to which [Thérèse] would be faithful to the Rule. It was hardly three weeks that she was in Carmel, and, thinking that she did not know how to find the Office alone, I wanted to keep her with me to teach her how to find the commemorations. But instead of taking advantage of this opportunity, she answered sweetly: "I thank you, I found them today. I would be happy to stay with you, but it is better that I deprive myself, for we are not at home!"[7]

"It is better that I deprive myself," Thérèse said, "for we are not at home." This is, I feel, a summary of Thérèse's attitude and of her way of going beyond simple bonds of natural affection. Marie also wrote: "During recreation she could often have found a place near us (her own sisters), but she sought in preference the company of those who tested her charity the most."[8]

Unfortunately, our time for this chapter is coming to its end. I thought that it was important to demonstrate how Thérèse was able to overcome her natural inclination toward her sisters, to open herself to a true and selfless fraternal charity toward all the nuns in the monastery; that's why I've dedicated so much time to the subject.

---

6 O'Mahony, ed., *St. Thérèse of Lisieux by Those who Knew Her*, 98.

7 See footnote 6 of *Letter* 49, in St. Thérèse, *Letters of St. Thérèse of Lisieux: General Correspondence*, vol. 1, 428.

8 O'Mahony, ed., *St. Thérèse of Lisieux by Those who Knew Her*, 98.

A FRATERNAL CHARITY FREED FROM EGOISTIC SELF-LOVE

Thérèse was clearly also very charitable toward her own family members. One can easily tell by briefly leafing through Thérèse's letters toward her family members, especially toward Céline. Thérèse was a source of comfort and spiritual elevation for Céline, especially during the painful and difficult years of their dear father's sickness. Céline and Léonie had even moved to an apartment, which they were renting, in Caen, to be closer to their father! And after his release from the psychiatric ward of the *Bon Sauveur* hospital, it was again Céline who most took care of Louis. Thérèse lavished Céline with an abundance of letters, in which she shared with her the intimate secrets of her soul and the spiritual lights she was receiving, and encouraged her; the same is to be said as regarding Céline's vocation to religious life, which Thérèse fiercely defended and protected through her letters, until she entered Carmel and became her novice. Céline's *Conseils et souvenirs*, which gather her notes taken during Thérèse's lessons during her novitiate, are extremely precious in that regard.

At the same time, Thérèse did not ignore the other members of her family, outside of Carmel. For example, her cousin Jeanne Guérin, married to Dr. Francis La Néele, who suffered for the fact of not being able to have children; Thérèse also encouraged Marie Guérin, Jeanne's sister, in her religious vocation. Marie would also enter into the Carmel of Lisieux and also became a novice under Thérèse's guidance. Thérèse's letters to her Uncle Isidore Guérin and his wife, her Aunt Madame Fournet were never lacking, especially for special recurrences or feast days, and she showed the most tender and filial affection and gratitude toward them.

Thérèse's letters to Léonie, by then a Visitandine nun, and also her poems and notes that she composed to console and encourage Céline in the first steps of her religious life in Carmel, could also be mentioned as a sign of Thérèse's special attention and charity toward her family members.

Most especially, all three *Manuscripts*—A, B, and C—which form the *Story of a Soul*, were requested by her family members: *Manuscript* A from Pauline Martin, at that time Mother Agnes of Jesus, through obedience; *Manuscript* B—although mostly already written—was requested by Sr. Marie of the Sacred Heart (Marie Pauline); and *Manuscript* C was furtively requested by Pauline Martin, by her convincing Mother Marie de Gonzague to order Thérèse to finish writing her childhood memories.

Thérèse wrote, as we mentioned before, to Mother Marie de Gonzague: "I can see with joy that in loving Him [Jesus] the heart expands and can give to those who are dear to it incomparably more tenderness than if it had concentrated upon one egotistical and unfruitful love." This pure and selfless charity of Thérèse, even to her sisters, is especially brilliant and inspiring in the notes taken by Sr. Agnes of Jesus (Pauline Martin) in what is now called the *Yellow Notebook*. Thérèse's affectionate but now totally free and God-driven love toward Pauline and all of her sisters, both blood sisters and religious sisters or nuns, is clearly visible in every page of the *Yellow Notebook*. I'll limit myself to one example: on July 29th, about two months before her death, Pauline wrote: "I was holding [Thérèse] up while they were arranging her pillows: 'I'm resting my head on the heart of my little Mother,'" Thérèse told her. And, that same afternoon, Pauline wrote: "For having rendered [Thérèse] a little service," she responded: "Thanks, Mamma!"

Thérèse's sacrifices and selfless love had widened her heart and allowed her to receive the immense love that Jesus was just waiting to pour into it. At the end of her life, in her human and spiritual maturity, that love overflowed abundantly and freely, without restraints or exertion, but naturally—or, should I say, supernaturally—to all around her, including of course her (blood) sisters.

FOURTH CHAPTER

St. Thérèse's charity toward sinners

INTRODUCTION: AN "INCLUSION." THE "THIRD PERIOD" OF THÉRÈSE'S LIFE.

Biblical scholars speak of an "inclusion," when a passage of the Sacred Scriptures contains a key word which is repeated in the first and last sentence of that particular section: the key word denotes a topic or underlying theme which characterizes that section of verses. "Inclusions" can be found in the span of a few sentences; at the beginning or end of a chapter, or even at the beginning and end of an entire book of the Bible. Borrowing this category from Biblical exegesis, it could also be applied, in a certain sense, to an important "chapter" in the "story" of Thérèse's life: what she herself defines as "the third period of my life, the most beautiful and the most filled with graces from Heaven" (Ms A, 45v°). This "third period" of Thérèse's life spans from her "conversion" on December 25th, 1886, up until her holy death on September 30th, 1897. That is, for the last eleven years of her earthly life, which of course lasted twenty-four years in all. As a matter of fact, as we'll see briefly now, the word and the theme of "sinners" is an important topic both upon her "conversion" and even on the last day of her life.

THÉRÈSE'S CONVERSION AND HER CHARITY TOWARD SINNERS: AN UNBREAKABLE TIE

To better understand Thérèse's charity and preoccupation for sinners, one must take into consideration the direct and consequent tie that Thérèse herself draws between her conversion on that famous Christmas Eve of 1886 and her desire to save souls. This is important to comprehend, because it gives the correct context and perspective—those given by Thérèse herself—regarding her charity for sinners.

We all remember the episode that marked Thérèse's "conversion": after returning from the Midnight Mass with her dear father Louis and her sisters, Thérèse was preparing herself, as was custom, to draw some Christmas gifts from the "magic shoes" that were awaiting her in the chimney corner. Her father Louis, tired from the long day, expressed some annoyance when seeing Thérèse's shoes at the fireplace, saying "Well, fortunately, this will be the last year!" Thérèse almost burst into tears, and Céline invited her to not descend the stairs right away, knowing how painful it was for Thérèse (still overly sensitive, from the time of her mother Zélie's death nine years before: cf. Ms A, 45r°). Instead, something happened: Thérèse herself describes this important grace with simple yet profound words:

> But Thérèse was no longer the same; Jesus had changed her heart! Forcing back my tears, I descended the stairs rapidly; controlling the poundings of my heart, I took my slippers and placed them in front of Papa, and withdrew all the objects joyfully. I had the happy appearance of a queen. Having regained his own cheerfulness, Papa was laughing; Céline believed it was all a dream! Fortunately, it was a sweet reality; Thérèse had discovered once again the strength of soul which she had lost at the age of four and a half, and she was to preserve it forever! (ibid.).

What was this "change of heart" that Thérèse refers to? First of all, it was the "strength of soul" which she had lost and finally found again. There were also other beneficial effects, however, of this special grace. Thérèse continues her account on the next page (that is, the back side of the forty-fifth page of a small black school notebook, the first of the two notebooks which would later compose that which is called her "*Manuscript* A"):

> On that *night of light* began the third period of my life, the most beautiful and the most filled with graces from Heaven. The work I had been unable to do in ten years was done by Jesus in one instant, contenting

> himself with my *good will* which was never lacking. I could say to Him like His apostles: "Master, I fished all night and caught nothing." More merciful to me than He was to His disciples, Jesus *took the net Himself*, cast it, and drew it in filled with fish. He made me a fisher of *souls*. I experienced a great desire to work for the conversion of sinners, a desire I hadn't felt so intensely before (Ms A, 45v°).

Thérèse describes the two principal and immediate effects of her "conversion" on that Christmas Eve. The first, again, was the regaining of her "strength of soul," lost since her mother's death; the second was—as she defines it—"a great desire to work for the conversion of sinners." Thérèse defines this grace as an accelerated process or turning point in her human and spiritual journey of maturation: she wrote on the page before: "It was December 25th, 1886, that I received the grace of leaving my childhood, in a word, the grace of my complete conversion" (Ms A, 45r°). And on the page before that, she had written: "I really don't know how I could entertain the thought of entering Carmel when I was still in the *swaddling clothes of a child*! God would have to work a little miracle to make me grow up in an instant, and this miracle He performed on that unforgettable Christmas day" (Ms A, 44v°).

THÉRÈSE'S CONVERSION: AN "EXODUS" FROM SELF-LOVE

It's interesting to consider that, for Thérèse, her conversion consisted in an instantaneous "exodus," as it were, from her childhood into a mature phase of her life. One could say that, from being a good but fussy child she suddenly became . . . a mother. She matured into adulthood and became a young woman, capable of generating life: in this case, divine life. In other words, she became a mother: a spiritual mother. She wrote, immediately after describing her "desire to work for the conversion of sinners": "I felt *charity* enter into my soul, and the need to forget myself and to please others; since then I've been happy!" (Ms A,

45v°). Does not maternity consist in this: forgetting oneself to please others? That is, unconditional and self-sacrificing love or charity? Such a love—such a divine love—generates life. Thérèse continued:

> I felt *charity* enter into my soul, and the need to forget myself and to please others; since then I've been happy! One Sunday, looking at a picture of Our Lord on the Cross, I was struck by the blood flowing from one of the divine hands. I felt a great pang of sorrow when thinking this blood was falling to the ground without anyone's hastening to gather it up. I was resolved to remain in spirit at the foot of the Cross and to receive the divine dew. I understood I was then to pour it out upon souls [...]. As yet, it was not the souls of priests that attracted me, but those of *great sinners*; I *burned* with the desire to snatch them from the eternal flames (ibid.).

SPIRITUAL MATERNITY IN THÉRÈSE

Thérèse herself, describing her desire to "work for the conversion of sinners," admits that it was a desire "I hadn't felt so intensely before." Her leaving her childhood and entering into a mature phase of life coincided with, therefore, or rather *brought to* a spiritual motherhood and an apostolic desire to save souls; this desire was increased shortly thereafter while meditating upon an image of our Crucified Lord. The Lord Himself was guiding Thérèse and making her quickly mature, by a series of events and graces tightly and consequently linked between themselves: shortly after the episode of her being struck by the image of Our Lord on the Cross, Thérèse was to hear about a great sinner, whom she would later define as "my sinner" and "my '*first child.*'" For Thérèse, sinners are thus "hers," that is, "her children," and, as we'll see later on, also her "brothers." That sinner was Henri Pranzini. Pranzini had murdered two women and a young girl in Paris. The episode had probably struck Thérèse in a particular way for an important reason: one of the victims, Marie Regnault, was an acquaintance of her uncle and cousins, that is, the

Guérin family. Thérèse had probably heard about the crime at her uncle's house.[1] Thérèse fervidly prayed for "her sinner" Pranzini and his conversion; she was certain that her desires—shared with Céline upon her insistence—would be granted. Thérèse followed Pranzini's trial through the newspaper, *La Croix*, that her father Louis loved to read. Thérèse wrote:

HENRI PRANZINI (1856–1887). IDENTIFICATION PHOTOGRAPH TAKEN BY THE POLICE AFTER HIS ARREST. THÉRÈSE CONSIDERED THIS CRIMINAL HER "FIRST CHILD."

> My prayer was answered to the letter! The day after [Pranzini's] execution I found the newspaper. "*La Croix*." I opened it quickly and what did I see? Ah! my tears betrayed my emotion and I was obliged to hide. Pranzini had not gone to confession. He had mounted the scaffold and was preparing to place his head in the formidable opening, when suddenly, seized by an inspiration, he turned, took hold of the *crucifix* the priest was holding out to him and *kissed* the *sacred wounds three times!* [...].

---

[1] See Ste. Thérèse, *Manuscrits autobiographiques*, 144 (cf. footnote regarding *Manuscript* A, 45v°, 23).

> I had obtained the "sign" I requested, and this sign was a perfect replica of the grace Jesus had given me when He attracted me to pray for sinners. Wasn't it before the *wounds of Jesus*, when seeing His divine *blood* flowing, that the thirst for souls had entered my heart? I wished to give them this *immaculate blood* to drink, this blood which was to purify them from their stains, and the lips of my "*first child*" *were* pressed to the sacred wounds! (Ms A, 46r°–46v°).

This was Thérèse's first experience of spiritual maternity: Pranzini was "her sinner," her "first child." He would not be the last. On the contrary! Thérèse continued:

> What an unspeakably sweet response [to my prayers]! After this unique grace [of Pranzini's conversion] my desire to save souls grew each day, and I seemed to hear Jesus say to me what he said to the Samaritan woman: "*Give me to drink!*" It was a true interchange of love: to souls I was giving the *blood of Jesus*, to Jesus I was offering these same souls refreshed by the *divine dew*. I slaked His thirst and the more I gave Him *to drink*, the more the thirst of my poor little soul increased, and it was this ardent thirst He was giving me as the most delightful drink of His love (Ms A, 46v°).

THÉRÈSE'S FRATERNAL CHARITY TOWARD SINNERS AFTER HER ENTRANCE INTO THE LISIEUX CARMEL

This "thirst" of Jesus for souls, shared by Him with Thérèse, would never be quenched . . . rather, it grew "each day," as she herself recounted. Let's move forward now, chronologically, to Thérèse's entrance into Carmel; or rather, to her definitive "entrance": that is, her Profession, on September 8th, 1890. Thérèse was, at that time, seventeen years of age. As was custom, Thérèse underwent a canonical examination or sort of interrogation before being admitted to her final vows. Thérèse describes this episode, writing:

> I had declared at the feet of Jesus-Victim, in the examination preceding my profession, what I had come to

> Carmel for: "I came to save souls and especially to pray for priests." When one wishes to attain a goal, one must use the means; Jesus made me understand that it was through suffering that He wanted to give me souls, and my attraction for suffering grew in proportion to its increase (Ms A, 69v°).

These words of Thérèse reveal two important attitudes or dispositions of her soul upon making her vows: (1) the desire to save souls; (2) the desire to suffer, inasmuch as—Thérèse understood—suffering was the means that Jesus had chosen for her to gain souls for Heaven. It was through suffering that she was to convert sinners. Suffering was the means, or instrument, that Jesus had chosen so that Thérèse could obtain the goals that Jesus Himself had inspired in her, calling her to Carmel, reassumed by Thérèse in the response that she gave during the canonical examination preceding her vows: "I came to save souls and especially to pray for priests."

A TELLING EXAMPLE: THÉRÈSE'S PRAYER 2, PROFESSION NOTE

A glance at Thérèse's *Profession Note*, that is, her *Prayer* 2, helps to shed ulterior light on Thérèse's internal dispositions during the moment of her Profession. Thérèse wrote:

> O Jesus, my divine spouse! [...].
>
> May Your will be done in me perfectly, and may I arrive at the place You have prepared for me...
>
> Jesus, allow me to save very many souls; let no soul be damned today; let all the souls in Purgatory be saved... Jesus, pardon me if I say anything I should not say. I want only to give You joy and to console You (Pr 2).

Thérèse's most intimate desires, on the day of her "wedding" with Jesus, are those of saving "very many souls"; hoping that "no soul be damned today," and that "all the souls in Purgatory be saved." In the *Catechism of the Catholic Church*, we are reminded that "Charity is the theological virtue by which we love God above all things for his own sake, and our neighbor as ourselves for the love of God."[2] Thérèse had this clear, and she would later understand it even more clearly, and write about it in her *Manuscript* C. Yet, her motives were already clear: "Jesus, pardon me if I say anything I should not say. I want only to give you joy and to console you." For Thérèse, the best way to give joy to Jesus and to console Him was by saving souls—the souls of sinners.

THE GRADUAL GROWTH OF THÉRÈSE'S FRATERNAL CHARITY TOWARD SINNERS

Although Thérèse felt a great "thirst" to save souls since her fourteenth year of age, especially after Pranzini's conversion, she only mentions "sinners" in her letters after her entrance into Carmel. A few months after her entrance, that is, on July 4th, 1888, she wrote to Sr. Agnes of Jesus (Pauline), in her *Letter* 54: "The grain of sand [Thérèse herself], in spite of its littleness, *wishes* to form beautiful Eternities; it wishes to form some for the souls of sinners, but, alas, it is still not little enough or light enough" (LT 54). Six months later, on January 6th, 1889, she wrote once more to Pauline, regarding sinners; in this *Letter* 74, we already see the important spiritual attitude and concepts that Thérèse would reiterate in her *Profession Note* almost two years later. She wrote:

> It is incredible how big my heart appears to me when I consider all earth's treasures. But when I consider Jesus, how little it appears to me! . . . I would so much like to love Him! . . . Love Him more than He has ever been loved! . . . My only desire is to do the will of Jesus always! To dry away the little tears that sinners make Him shed . . . Oh! I do not WANT Jesus to have any sorrow. On the day of my espousals, I would like to convert *all* the sinners of this earth and to save all the souls in Purgatory!. . . (LT 74).

When Thérèse refers, here, to the day of her "espousals," she is not speaking yet of her Profession, but rather of her

[2] *Catechism of the Catholic Church*, no. 1822.

Clothing Ceremony, which took place on January 10th, 1889, that is, four days later. Thérèse had entered into her retreat in preparation for the Taking of the Habit the day before, on January 5th. All was silence and aridity; her father's sickness worried her, and the "creatures" around her "riddled" her with "little holes" and "pin-pricks" (cf. LT 74). However, in this context of suffering, her faith and her love was increasing: "I would so much like to love Him! . . . Love Him more than He has ever been loved! . . . My only desire is to do the will of Jesus always!" Her love of God was increasing; but also her love for neighbor, particularly sinners: "My only desire is [. . .] to dry away the little tears that sinners make Him shed [. . .]. On the day of my espousals, I would like to convert *all* the sinners of this earth and to save all the souls in Purgatory!"

HYACINTHE LOYSON: ANOTHER "PRANZINI" FOR THÉRÈSE

Jumping forward in time . . . and coming to the summer following Thérèse's Profession, Thérèse heard of another great sinner. In a certain sense, this man could be considered a "second Pranzini" for Thérèse, although she was more discreet in his regards—a discretion imposed by the "taboo" surrounding him. I'm referring to Fr. Hyacinthe Loyson. The Carmel of Lisieux Archives website describes him with the following words:

> Successively Sulpician, Dominican novice, then Carmelite for ten years, Father Hyacinthe, a famous preacher, had attracted crowds to Notre Dame de Paris before publicly breaking with his Order in a letter dated September 20th, 1869, in opposition to the teachings of [Pope] Pius IX and above all to papal infallibility. In another public letter on July 30th, 1870, he declared his definitive withdrawal from the Church, and on September 3rd, 1872, he married Mrs. Meriman, an American Protestant widow whom he had converted to Catholicism four years earlier. He became the promoter of "The Church of the Free Spirit."[3]

[3] https://archives.carmeldelisieux.fr/personnage/loyson-hyacinthe/ (the translation is mine).

Thérèse, in her correspondence and even in her conversation, never pronounced his name: it was forbidden to speak of him in the Lisieux monastery. She spoke and wrote of him anyway, but in code language and without pronouncing his name. On July 8th, 1891, writing to Céline, she expressed the desire to obtain Fr. Loyson's conversion:

> Yes, dear Céline, suffering alone can give birth to souls for Jesus . . . Is it surprising that we are so favored, we whose only desire is to save a soul that seems to be lost forever?. . . The details interested me very much,

FR. HYACINTH LOYSON, O.C.D.
(BEFORE LEAVING THE ORDER AND THE CATHOLIC CHURCH)

> while making my heart beat very fast . . . But I shall give you some other details that are not any more consoling. The unfortunate prodigal went to Coutances where he started over again the lectures given at Caen. It appears he intends to travel throughout France in this way . . . Céline . . . [. . .]. His wife follows him everywhere. Dear Céline, he is really culpable, more culpable than any other sinner ever was who was converted. But cannot Jesus do once what He has not ever done? And if He were not to desire it, would He have placed in the heart of His poor little spouses a desire that He could not realize?. . . No, it is certain that He desires more than we do to bring back this poor stray sheep to the fold (LT 129).

Thérèse was struck by the fact that Hyacinthe Loyson had been a (famous) Carmelite preacher; in the same *Letter* 129, she refers to him as "our brother" and as "a son of the Blessed Virgin." Thérèse would never forget to pray for his conversion, and even offered her Last Communion (August 19th, 1897) for him. In January of 1911, the Carmel of Lisieux sent Hyacinthe Loyson a copy of the *Story of a Soul.* He responded, stating: "I was touched, very much touched, by many of the things I read in this book. I must add [however] that I am far from being convinced." He would remain "far from being convinced" until his death. However, his last words—I feel—somewhat resemble Pranzini's last gesture (of kissing the crucifix). Loyson died whispering his last words: "My sweet Jesus!"[4] Had Thérèse, on earth and later from Heaven, obtained his conversion as well? I believe so.

THÉRÈSE'S POEMS: AN EXPRESSION OF HER FRATERNAL CHARITY TOWARD SINNERS

A few years later, in her masterpiece poem, *Living on Love!*, that is, her *Poem* 17, Thérèse wrote:

> Living on Love is wiping your Face,
> It's obtaining the pardon of sinners.
> O God of Love! May they return to your grace,
> And may they forever bless your Name...
> Even in my heart the blasphemy resounds.
> To efface it, I always want to sing:
> I adore and love your Sacred Name.
> I live on Love!... (P 17).

In her poetry, Thérèse felt free to express her most intimate sentiments. No surprise, then, that the category of "sinners" returns to her pen as a "refrain" throughout her poetry. A few examples will suffice: firstly, her *Poem* 21, *Canticle of a Soul Having Found the Place of its Rest*, written for her cousin Marie Guérin's entrance into Carmel (August 15th,

[4] See St. Thérèse of the Child Jesus and of the Holy Face, *Letters of St. Thérèse of Lisieux: General Correspondence*, vol. 2 (1890–1897), transl. J. Clarke, 730–31.

1895). The introductory notes to her *Poem* 21 comment: "It was the custom for a new postulant to 'sing something' for the community on the evening of her entrance [...], [and] she was gifted with a beautiful soprano voice. Thérèse wanted to show it off [...] and this song expressed a spiritual plan of action for the new arrival."[5] Thérèse, in fact, composed most of her poetry—almost all of her poems—to be sung, adapting her verses to the rhythm and melody of well-known songs, mostly Church-related. In the first verse, her cousin Marie sung, as Thérèse had written:

> O Jesus! on this day when you have broken my bonds...
> In the blessed Order of the Virgin Mary
> I shall be able to find true wealth.
> Lord, if I have left my dear family,
> You will know how to heap heavenly favors on them,
> And to me, you will give the pardon of sinners...(P 21).

For Thérèse, the pardon of sinners is the reward and, I would say, the "dower gift" for her cousin Marie's entrance into Carmel and the sacrifice of her family and friends. The pardon of sinners is, again for Thérèse, one of the main reasons for entering Carmel, as she had expressed herself in the canonical examination preceding her own Profession.

Two months later (on October 21st, 1895), for her sister Céline, who had asked Thérèse to compose a poem reminding Jesus of all that she (Céline) had sacrificed for Him, Thérèse reversed the logic of her sister's request and wrote a poem based on Jesus's sacrifices for Céline: her *Poem* 24, *Jesus, My Beloved, Remember!* In stanza 16 of this poem, Thérèse wrote:

> Remember the Angel's feast,
> Remember Heaven's harmony
> And the joy of the sublime hosts
> When a sinner raises his eyes to you.
> Ah! I want to increase that great joy.
> Jesus, I want to pray unceasingly for sinners.

[5] *The Poetry of Saint Thérèse of Lisieux*, transl. Kinney, 111.

That I came to Carmel
To fill your beautiful Heaven,
Remember... (P 24).

Further on, in the same *Poem* 24, Thérèse wrote: "I am a virgin, O Jesus! yet what a mystery./ When I unite myself to you, I am the mother of souls./ The virginal flowers/ Who save sinners,/ Remember." And, in stanza 31, she wrote: "Remember that on earth I want/ To console you for the forgetfulness of sinners./ My only Love, grant my prayer./ Ah! give me a thousand hearts to love you."

In Thérèse's *Poem* 46, instead, she anticipates what she would later write: for Thérèse, sinners are her "brothers." "During my short life I want/ To save my brothers, the sinners/ O Fair Angel of the Homeland,/ Give me holy fervor./ I have nothing but my sacrifices/ And my austere poverty./ With your celestial delights,/ Offer them to the Trinity" (P 46).[6]

THÉRÈSE'S PLAYS: ANOTHER EXPRESSION OF HER CHARITABLE PREOCCUPATION FOR SINNERS

Although there's no time now to thoroughly deepen this point, it must be said that Thérèse develops her concept of God's mercy for sinners, and their conversion, in her *Plays* or *Pious Recreations*, as well. It is a recurrent theme in her *Plays* 2, 3, 4, 5, 6, and 8. Thérèse followed the common misconception of her time that Mary Magdalene was the same Mary, sister of Lazarus and Martha; in her *Play* 4, *Jesus at Bethany*, the theme of the penitent Mary (Magdalene) recurs frequently. In their dialogue, put into verses, Jesus says to Mary (Magdalene): "If I love the pure/ And brilliant fires of dawn/ Oh Mary! I also love/ A beautiful radiant evening./ My goodness without equal/ Would like that the sinner/ And the virginal soul/ Rest on My heart" (PR 4). Whereas, in Thérèse's *Play* 2, *The Angel at Jesus's Manger*, written for Christmas 1894, one can already see, between the lines, the first strokes

[6] *Poem* 46, *To my Guardian Angel* (January 1897), in *The Poetry of Saint Thérèse of Lisieux*, transl. Kinney, 189. (The translation is mine, in part.)

of her pen regarding her "Little Way." At the end of the *Pious Recreation*, the "Angel of the Last Judgment," present at the Nativity Scene together with various other angels, cries out (or rather, sings):

> Jesus, supreme beauty! Have You then forgotten
> That sinners must be punished at the end?...
> Have You forgotten, in Your extreme love
> That the number of the impious is countless?...
> At the judgment, I shall punish crime.
> I want to wipe out all the ungrateful...
> My sword is ready! ... Jesus, sweet victim!...
> My sword is ready!! ... I'll know how to avenge
> You!!!... (2*x*) (PR 2).

The Child Jesus replies to the Angel of the Last Judgment with some surprising words, which seem to flow out directly and spontaneously from Thérèse's heart:

> O Beautiful angel! Lay down your sword.
> It is not for you to judge
> The nature that I raise up
> And have desired to redeem.
> It is I, named Jesus,
> Who will judge the world!
> The fecund dew of My blood
> Will purify all My elect.
> Do you know that faithful souls
> Will console Me forever
> For the blasphemies of the unfaithful
> By a simple look of love?...
> Also, in the Holy Fatherland,
> My elect will be glorified.
> By giving them My life
> I will make them like unto *gods!*... (ibid.).

THÉRÈSE'S *PRAYERS* FOR SINNERS

Not only in her *Plays*, but also in her *Prayers*, Thérèse refers often to sinners. I've already mentioned, various times, Thérèse's *Prayer* 2, *Profession Note* (September 8th, 1890). Her *Prayer* 4, *Homage to the Most Blessed Trinity* (February

1894), is also very significant: written to help Sr. Martha of Jesus, one of her novices, Thérèse "bends down," as it were, putting herself graciously in the same spiritual place as her novice, who still needed to count her acts of charity and prayer. Thérèse was far from such a spirituality! Yet, she knew that "God leads each soul on a different path," as Céline would later testify. The whole *Prayer* 4 is focused, practically, on reparation for sinners' misdeeds and the desire to console God in return. Thérèse wrote:

> O my God, behold us as we bow before You. We come to beseech You for the grace of working for Your glory.
>
> The blasphemies of sinners have sounded painfully in our ears. We wish to console You and to repair for the insults that souls redeemed by You make You suffer. O adorable Trinity! we want to form a *concert* of all the little sacrifices we will make for Your love. For fifteen days, we will offer You the song of the little birds of Heaven who unceasingly praise You and reproach men and women for their ingratitude. We will offer You also, O my God! the melody of musical instruments and we hope that our souls may merit to be a melodious lyre You can play to console Yourself for the indifference of so many souls who do not think of You. Likewise, for eight days we want to collect *diamonds* and precious stones to repair for the eagerness of poor mortals who pursue passing riches without dreaming of those of eternity. O my God! grant us the grace to be more vigilant in seeking sacrifices than those who do not love You are in their pursuit of worldly goods.
>
> Finally, for eight days your children will gather the *fragrance* of flowers. By doing this they wish to make amends for all that priestly and religious souls make You suffer by their offenses. O blessed Trinity, grant us to be faithful and give us the grace to possess You after the exile of this life . . . Amen (Pr 4).[7]

[7] *Prayer* 4, *Homage to the Most Blessed Trinity*, in St. Thérèse of Lisieux, *The Prayers of Saint Thérèse of Lisieux*, transl. Aletheia Kane, O.C.D. (Washington, D.C.: ICS Publications, 1997), 43.

In a similar context, Thérèse found herself again complying to the spirituality of her time, so as to prepare a booklet for a fellow nun in the monastery, Sr. Marie-Madeleine, in preparation for her Profession. Thérèse was inspired by the little booklet that her sister Pauline (Sr. Agnes of Jesus) had made for her in preparation for her First Communion. Even at that time—judging by Thérèse's recount of her First Communion—she was far beyond this sort of spirituality. When Thérèse was composing this booklet for Sr. Marie-Madeleine, in October of 1894, she was already poring over the Sacred Scriptures contained in *Céline's Notebook* and had just discovered (or was about to discover) her "Little Way" with a greater clarity and spiritual impact than ever. Although "light years," so to speak, beyond her nun-sister, Sr. Marie-Madeleine, Thérèse conforms herself to her tastes and produces this little booklet, in which Sr. Marie-Madeleine was to gather "flowers" (sacrifices) and express her "aspirations" (spontaneous prayers and acts of love toward God). Sr. Marie-Madeleine gathered 180 "flowers" or sacrifices, and expressed 2,924 "aspirations," probably recited in decades, like the Rosary, in two weeks.[8] On the back of the sixth page, entitled "White Peonies," Thérèse wrote: "O my God, look at the Face of Jesus and count all sinners among the elect." In her next *Prayer*, her *Prayer* 6, *Act of Oblation to Merciful Love*, written in June of 1895, Thérèse would express a similar concept, but this time applied to herself: "Since You loved me so much as to give me Your only Son as my Savior and my Spouse, the infinite treasures of His merits are mine. I offer them to You with gladness, begging You to look on me only through the Face of Jesus and in His Heart burning with Love." In fact, in Thérèse's *Prayers*, sinners and the Face of Jesus are often related. In her *Prayer* 12, *Consecration to the Holy Face*, recited together with Sr. Geneviève of the Holy Face (Céline Martin) and Sr. Marie of the Trinity, her two novices, on August 6th, 1896, Thérèse wrote:

[8] See St. Thérèse of Lisieux, *The Prayers of Saint Thérèse of Lisieux*, transl. Kane, 51.

> *O Adorable Face of Jesus!* [...] Our souls understand Your language of *love*; we want to dry Your *gentle Face* and to console You for the forgetfulness of the wicked. In their eyes You are still as one hidden; they look upon You as an object of contempt...
>
> *O Face* more beautiful than the lilies and roses of springtime! You are not hidden from our eyes ... The *Tears* that veil Your *divine look* seem to us like *precious Diamonds* which we want to collect to buy the souls of our brothers and sisters with their infinite value.
>
> *Souls, Lord,* we need *souls* ... above all *the souls of apostles and martyrs* so that through them we might *inflame* all poor sinners *with Your Love* (Pr 12).

THÉRÈSE'S LOVE FOR SINNERS, UNTIL THE END

It is important to note that Thérèse calls sinners, in her *Prayer 12*, *Consecration to the Holy Face*, her "brothers and sisters." She thus anticipates what she would later write in her *Poem 46*, *To my Guardian Angel* (January 1897) and, especially, when recounting her "trial of faith." In June of 1897, Thérèse wrote the following lines:

> Your child, however, O Lord, has understood Your divine light, and she begs pardon for her brothers. She is resigned to eat the bread of sorrow as long as You desire it; she does not wish to rise up from this table filled with bitterness at which poor sinners are eating until the day set by You. Can she not say in her name and in the name of her brothers, *"Have pity on us, O Lord, for we are poor sinners!"* Oh! Lord, send us away justified. May all those who were not enlightened by the bright flame of faith one day see it shine. O Jesus! if it is needful that the table soiled by them be purified by a soul who loves You, then I desire to eat this bread of trial at this table until it pleases You to bring me into Your bright kingdom. The only grace I ask of You is that I never offend You (Ms C, 6r°).

I believe that this experience of Thérèse, this "trial of faith," was not for her own purification; but rather, for the purification of many: as Thérèse herself would write about a month later, "Your Love has gone before me, and it has grown with me, and now it is an abyss whose depths I cannot fathom [...]. O my Jesus, it is perhaps an illusion but it seems to me that You cannot fill a soul with more love than the love with which You have filled mine" (Ms C, 35r°). A soul impacted, penetrated, imbued, and transformed by God's love like the soul of Thérèse, was already purified ... Her sufferings were, at that point in her life, a purification for others. God's charity in her had grown, so much so to become "an abyss whose depths I cannot fathom"; and her charity had grown, even to the point of an intimate participation in the innocent sufferings of Christ for the sins of others: He is the Lamb of God, Who takes upon Himself the sins of the world. Thérèse's charity, indeed, participated in that of God's, and thus knew no bounds. At the end of her life, on the last day of her life, Thérèse herself would marvel at the extreme sufferings that she was undergoing, and could find only the following explanation: "Never would I have believed it was possible to suffer so much! Never! Never! I cannot explain this except by the ardent desires I have had to save souls" (CJ, September 30th).[9]

[9] *Yellow Notebook*, September 30th, 1897 (the day of Thérèse's holy death).

FIFTH CHAPTER
St. Thérèse's charity toward priests

INTRODUCTION: PRIESTS AND THE MARTIN FAMILY

For those of you who may be priests, this topic is particularly engaging and profitable; but, in reality, it is for all faithful. Thérèse had a great love for everyone; but she had a special charity for priests. How did she get to know them? What did she do for them, to express her spiritual charity…? Without further ado, let's start looking for some answers to these important questions.

Thérèse was certainly familiar with priests from her most early infancy: her parents and her siblings would go to Mass every Sunday. Actually, as Céline later testified in the Process for her sister Thérèse's beatification: "Both my parents [Louis and Zélie Martin] went to early Mass every day, and received Communion as often as they could […]. Above all, he [Louis Martin] had great esteem for priests."[1] At Sunday Mass—after her mother Zélie's death—Thérèse loved to sit next to her "King," that is, her dear father Louis, during Mass. She later recounted her childhood experiences of Mass together with her father:

> All along the way to church and even in the church Papa's little queen held his hand. Her place was by his side, and when we had to go down into the body of the church to listen to the sermon, two chairs had to be found side by side. This wasn't too difficult, for everyone seemed to think it so wonderful to see such a *handsome* old man with such a *little daughter* that they went out of their way to give them their places […].
>
> I wasn't too disturbed at being looked at by people. I listened attentively to the sermons which I understood very poorly. The first I *did understand* and

---

[1] Cf. Mother Geneviève of the Holy Face's (= Céline Martin's) testimony on Thérèse, in O'Mahony, ed., *St. Thérèse of Lisieux by Those who Knew Her*, 110.

> which *touched me deeply* was a sermon on the Passion preached by Father Ducellier and since then I've understood all the others. When the preacher spoke about St. Teresa, Papa leaned over and whispered: "Listen carefully, little queen, he's talking about your Patroness." I did listen carefully, but I looked more frequently at Papa than at the preacher, for his *handsome* face said so much to me! His eyes, at times, were filled with *tears* which he tried in vain to stop; he seemed no longer held by earth, so much did his soul love to lose itself in the eternal truths (Ms A, 17r°–17v°).

We must note that Thérèse remembered—many years later—the name of the priest who had given the first homily that she, as a child, had understood: Fr. Ducellier. From then on, Thérèse affirms, she understood all the other homilies as well. She also states that she would listen carefully to the homilies. Of course, she was more impressed by her dear father, whom she looked at "more frequently" than at the preacher: "His *handsome* face said so much to me! His eyes, at times, were filled with *tears*."

Besides going to Mass every Sunday (and sometimes during the week, as well), the Martin and Guérin families, whom Thérèse grew up with, certainly spoke of the Pope, bishops, and priests, as well as other topics tied to their Catholic faith. (Later on in life, her Uncle Isidore Guérin, Zélie's brother, started to write for the Catholic apologetical newspaper *Le Normand.*[2]) Céline (Sr. Geneviève of the Holy Face) would later testify in the Apostolic Process for Thérèse's canonization regarding her father Louis Martin's respect for priests: "His respect for priests was so great that I've never seen anything like it. I remember that, being little, I used to think that priests were gods, so accustomed was I to seeing them placed outside the common rank."[3]

---

[2] Cf. https://archives.carmeldelisieux.fr/en/personnage/isidore-guerin/ (accessed on April 1st, 2025).

[3] See Sr. Geneviève of the Holy Face's testimony in *Procés de Béatification et Canonisation de Sainte Thérèse de l'Enfant-Jésus et de la Sainte-Face* (II—Procès Apostolique et petit procès pour la recherche des écrits de la sainte) (Rome: Teresianum, 1976), 256.

THE PRESENCE OF PRIESTS IN THÉRÈSE'S CHILDHOOD

Thérèse knew about priests not only through the Martin homestead; during her lessons with Madame Pâpinau—her private tutor as a child—her mother Madame Cochain would often receive guests at home. "Who could believe it! In this antiquely furnished room, surrounded as I was by text books and copybooks, I was often present at the visits of all types of persons; priests, ladies, young girls, etc." (Ms A, 39v°–40r°).

Priests would also pay visits to the Martins. We know it from Thérèse:

> It was on Wednesday also that Father Ducellier came to pay a visit. Victoire told him nobody was home except Thérèse, and so he came out into the *kitchen* to see me and look over my homework; I was very proud to receive my *confessor*, for I had made my first confession to him a short time before. What a sweet memory for me! (Ms A, 16v°).

Speaking of Thérèse's confessor, Fr. Ducellier—the same priest whose homily she had understood, for the first time in her life—it's worth mentioning Thérèse's First Confession, which she herself recounts:

> Oh! dear Mother,[4] with what care you prepared me for my first confession, telling me it was not to a man but to God I was about to tell my sins; I was very much convinced of this truth. I made my confession in a great spirit of faith, even asking you if I had to

[4] We must remember that Thérèse's *Manuscript* A was addressed to her sister Pauline, whom she had chosen as her "second mother" on the day of their mother Zélie's funeral, when Thérèse was only four years old. Pauline had prepared Thérèse for her First Confession (in person) and her First Communion (from Carmel, with a booklet especially made for the occasion). Thérèse called Pauline "Mother" not only because she had chosen her as her "second mother," but also because she had been elected Prioress of Carmel, and it was she—Mother Agnes of Jesus (Pauline)—who had told Thérèse to write down her childhood memories. Thérèse obeyed, writing in two notebooks (in the time period between January 1895 to January 1896) what would later be called her *Manuscript* A, which is the first section of the *Story of a Soul*.

FR. ALCIDE DUCELLIER (ASSOCIATE PASTOR OF ST. PETER'S CATHEDRAL IN LISIEUX FROM 1877 TO 1884)

tell Father Ducellier I loved him with all my heart as it was to God in person I was speaking.

Well instructed in all I had to say and do, I entered the confessional and knelt down. On opening the grating Father Ducellier saw no one. I was so little my head was below the arm-rest. He told me to stand up. Obeying instantly, I stood and faced him directly in order to see him perfectly, and I made my confession like a *big girl* and received his blessing with *great devotion* for you had told me that at the moment he gave me absolution the *tears of Jesus* were going to purify my soul. I remember the first exhortation directed to me. Father encouraged me to be devout to the Blessed Virgin and I promised myself to redouble my tenderness for her. Coming out of the confessional I was so happy and light-hearted that I had never felt so much joy in my soul. Since then I've gone to confession on all the great feasts, and it was truly a *feast* for me each time (Ms A, 16v°–17r°).

Thérèse had frequent contacts, then, with priests. As a matter of fact, it was a priest who taught her catechism, in preparation for her First Communion: Fr. Domin. "I listened with great attention to the instructions Father Domin was giving us, evening writing up a summary of them" (Ms A, 34r°). "On the evening of the great day [of my First Communion], I received absolution for the second time. My general confession left a great peace in my soul, and God did not permit the lightest cloud to come and trouble me" (Ms A, 34v°), Thérèse continued. She recalls another priest as well, when writing of her First Communion:

> I had written to Father Pichon to recommend myself to his prayers and to tell him that soon I would be a Carmelite and he would be my director. (This is what happened four years later, since it was to him I opened my soul.) Marie gave me a *letter from him*, and my happiness was complete! All these good things came to me together. What pleased me very much in his letter was this sentence: "Tomorrow, I will ascend the altar to say Mass for you and your [sister] Pauline" (Ms A, 34v°).

Father Pichon was effectively Thérèse's spiritual director even during her years in Carmel. Too bad that he burned all of Thérèse's letters, as was his habit with all of the people he followed as a spiritual director! Probably an excessive scrupulosity, on his behalf, so that others could not chance upon the letters. Thérèse would write to him faithfully once a month, but he would only respond about once a year! That's why Thérèse would often say that her real spiritual director was Jesus. And so it was...

THÉRÈSE'S PILGRIMAGE TO ROME: "I UNDERSTOOD MY VOCATION IN ITALY"

Thérèse's experience of priests, as a child, was extremely positive. Her month-long trip to Italy, together with 195 pilgrims—of whom 73 were priests[5]—was fundamental and, I would say, "eye-opening" for Thérèse. Together with her

[5] Sainte Thérèse, *Manuscrits autobiographiques*, p. 177, at the note to 55v°, 23, *au milieu de la noblesse.*

dear father Louis and her sister Céline, from November 4th to December 2nd, 1887, Thérèse journeyed as a pilgrim to Rome. Thérèse was fourteen years old. Her goal: "have a word" from Pope Leo XIII. It was the Pope's fifty-year-anniversary or Jubilee of priesthood ordination. Thérèse was determined to gain his permission to enter Carmel at only fifteen years of age.

Although "scrutinized" by Msgr. Révérony, by order of Bishop Hugonin, so as to have a better idea of the truth of Thérèse's vocation, Thérèse kept to her true self. No masks.[6] Thérèse herself would later write:

> Céline and I were intrepid; we were always the first and were following the bishop closely in order to see everything pertaining to the relics of the saints and hear the explanations given by the guides [...]. And it was like this everywhere, except in those places reserved to dignitaries and then we did not follow His Excellency (Ms A, 58v°).

Besides following the bishop closely, Thérèse records other bold gestures of hers and Céline's, her "intrepid" and inseparable companion: climbing to the very *top* of the bell tower of the Cathedral of Milan (cf. ibid.); sneaking into the Colosseum's combat area so as to kiss the soil that had been bathed by the blood of martyrs (cf. Ms A, 60v°–61r°); or slipping down together "to the bottom of the ancient tomb of St. Cecilia and taking some earth which was sanctified by her presence" (cf. Ms A, 61v°).

It was precisely during this long pilgrimage, exhilarating for all of the new and beautiful landscapes and cities, as well as spiritual attractions, that Thérèse also discovered the sense of her future vocation as a Carmelite. She would later write:

> The second experience I had relates to priests. Having never lived close to them, I was not able to understand the principal aim of the reform of Carmel. To pray for

[6] The observation is Guy Gaucher's: see his excellent biography of Thérèse: *Sainte Thérèse de Lisieux (1873–1897)*, 263.

> sinners attracted me, but to pray for the souls of priests whom I believed to be as pure as crystal seemed puzzling to me! (Ms A, 56r°).

It's worth noting that this image of priests being "as pure as crystal" probably derived from a book on St. Francis of Assisi that Thérèse had read as a child. In that book, the author relates that "One day, while [St. Francis] was praying, an Angel appeared to him and, showing him a vase full of water clearer than crystal, said to him: 'Look, Francis: the soul of a priest must be even more pure [than this crystal-pure water].'"[7]

THÉRÈSE CONTINUED WRITING IN HER *MANUSCRIPT* A:

> I understood *my vocation* in *Italy* and that's not going too far in search of such useful knowledge. I lived in the company of many *saintly priests* for a month and I learned that, though their dignity raises them above the angels, they are nevertheless weak and fragile men. If *holy priests*, whom Jesus in His Gospel calls the *"salt of the earth,"* show in their conduct their extreme need for prayers, what is to be said of those who are tepid? Didn't Jesus say too: *"If the salt loses its savor, wherewith will it be salted?"*
>
> How beautiful is the vocation, O Mother, which has as its aim the *preservation* of the *salt* destined for souls! This is Carmel's vocation since the sole purpose of our prayers and sacrifices is to be the apostle of the *apostles*. We are to pray for them while they are preaching to souls through their words and especially their example. I must stop here, for were I to continue I would never come to an end! (ibid.).

"I must stop here," Thérèse writes, "for were I to continue I would never come to an end!" These words of Thérèse are comforting for us priests. It means that her love, her prayer, and her care for priests is unlimited!

---

[7] Cf. Ste. Thérèse, *Manuscrits autobiographiques*, 178. See the footnote regarding *Manuscript* A, 56r°, 14: *plus pures que le cristal.*

SOME DELUSIONS...

Thérèse was, unfortunately, disappointed by the Vicar General of the Bishop of Bayeux, Msgr. Révérony. He had "blocked" her and impeded her from expressing herself fully to the Pope. Thérèse recounted that very same evening, in her letter to Pauline:

> The pope was seated on a large chair, very high. M. Révérony was very close to him; he was looking at the pilgrims who were passing in front of the pope after kissing his foot, and he was saying a word about some of them. You can imagine how my heart was beating when seeing my turn come, but I did not want to return to my place without having spoken to the pope. I said what you were telling me in your letter but not all, for M. Révérony did not give me time. He said immediately: "Most Holy Father, this is a child who wants to enter Carmel at fifteen, but the superiors are considering the matter at this moment." (The good pope is so old that one would say he is dead; I would never have pictured him like this. He can hardly say anything. It is M. Révérony who talks.) I would have liked to be able to explain my business, but there was no way. The Holy Father said simply: "If God wills it, you will enter." Then they made me pass into another room. Oh! Pauline, I cannot tell you what I felt. I was crushed. I felt I was abandoned, and, then, I am so far, so far... I was crying a lot when writing this letter; my heart is heavy. However, God cannot give me trials that are above my strength. He has given me the courage to bear this trial. Oh! it is very great... But, Pauline, I am the Child Jesus's little ball; if He wishes to break His toy, He is free. Yes, I will all that He wills (LT 36).[8]

Thérèse's audacious request to Pope Leo XIII did not go unobserved. A local newspaper of the Lisieux area, *L'Univers*, reported the incident. The whole pilgrimage knew of Thérèse's secret. While Thérèse and Céline went to Naples and Pompei

---

[8] *Letter* 36 (to Sr. Agnes of Jesus; November 20th, 1887), in St. Thérèse, *The Letters of St. Thérèse of Lisieux: General Correspondence*, vol. 1, 353.

in the following days, Mr. Martin remained in Rome. Three days after Thérèse's audience with the Pope, the "winds" turned slightly to her favor.[9] Thérèse herself recounts:

> A few days after the audience with the Holy Father, Papa, having gone to see good Brother Simeon, found Father Révérony there, who was very friendly. Papa chided him gaily for not having aided me in my *difficult undertaking*, then he told his queen's story to Brother Simeon. The venerable old man listened to his recital with much interest, even took down notes, and said with emotion: "One doesn't see this in Italy!" I believe this interview made a good impression on Father Révérony; afterward he never ceased proving to me that he was *finally* convinced of my vocation (Ms A, 64v°).

Thérèse had the opportunity of speaking with Fr. Révérony two times on their trip back to Lisieux—in a carriage and on a bus—and both times he was friendly and acquiescing. "I was by his side, on another occasion, on a bus, and he was even more friendly, promising *to do all he could to have me enter Carmel*" (ibid.), Thérèse recounts. Upon her return to Lisieux, Thérèse wrote to Bishop Hugonin requesting to enter Carmel; on December 28th, 1887 he responded affirmatively. He had left the question in the hands of the Prioress, Mother Marie de Gonzague, who fortunately supported Thérèse's precocious vocation. However, it was decided that Thérèse enter only after the Lenten season, considering the hardships of fasting and other penances in the monastery.

PERMISSION TO ENTER CARMEL

Finally, the happy day arrived! On April 9th, 1888, Thérèse entered Carmel amongst the tears of her family members and the blessing of her dear father Louis. "I knelt down before my matchless father for his blessing, and to give it to me he placed *himself on his knees* and blessed me, tears flowing down his cheeks." Not all bystanders were so graceful and full

[9] Cf. Gaucher, *Saint Thérèse of Lisieux: The Story of a Life*, 94.

of love . . . The canonical Superior of the Lisieux Carmel, Msgr. Delatroëtte, had already expressed his desire that Thérèse enter Carmel at twenty-one years of age, and not before. He regretted the fact that the bishop had given permission to the Mother Prioress to choose for herself, as regards to Thérèse's entrance.[10] In front of Thérèse, her father and relatives, and the whole community of the nuns, Msgr. Delatroëtte said:

> Well! Reverend Mothers, you can sing a *Te Deum*! As the bishop's delegate I give you this fifteen-year-old child whose entrance you have wished for. I hope she does not disappoint your hopes, but I remind you that if she does you alone will bear the responsibility.[11]

Msgr. Delatroëtte had already expressed his doubts directly to Thérèse a few months before her entrance, in a letter. He wrote: "I cannot stop myself from regretting that you have pushed so forcefully to enter [Carmel]; I fear that later on you and your sisters will repent [of this choice]."[12] Thérèse never mentions, in any of her writings, Delatroëtte's severe and ice-cold words.

As we have seen, Thérèse suffered by the hands of multiple ecclesiastical figures before (and during) her entrance into Carmel: Bishop Hugonin, the Vicar General Msgr. Révérony, the Superior Msgr. Delatroëtte. Yet, she never harbored resentment toward them, nor does she denigrate them in her memoirs to her sister Pauline. She well could have, as Thérèse believed that only her sister Pauline (Mother Agnes of Jesus) would have read her story. "It is for *you alone* I am writing the story of the *little flower* gathered by Jesus. I will talk freely and without any worries as to the numerous digressions I will make. A mother's heart understands her child even when it

---

[10] See Gaucher, *Saint Thérèse of Lisieux: The Story of a Life*, 95–97.

[11] Gaucher, *Saint Thérèse of Lisieux: The Story of a Life*, 104. The quotation is from Pauline Martin's testimony in the Apostolic Process for Thérèse's canonization, 141.

[12] *LC* 74 (January 30th, 1888), in Ste. Thérèse de l'Enfant-Jésus et de la Sainte-Face, *Édition critique des Œuvres Complètes, en huit volumes*, 2nd edn., "Nouvelle Édition du Centenaire" (Lonrai : Éditions du Cerf/Desclée De Brouwer, 1992): *Correspondance générale*, vol. 1 (1877–1890), 2nd edn., 337.

can but stammer, and so I'm sure of being understood by you, who formed my heart, offering it up to Jesus!" (Ms A, 3v°), Thérèse wrote in the first pages of her *Story of a Soul*. This shows an attitude of Thérèse that she cultivated from the beginning to the end of her life. A sincere and unresentful charity toward all, and in a particular way toward priests. And, as well, a positive and compassionate attitude toward her own weaknesses and to those of others. She would later write to Fr. Bellière, in one of her last letters to him: "You must know me only imperfectly to fear that a detailed account of your faults may diminish the tenderness I have for your soul" (LT 261).[13] (It's worth mentioning that the Bishop Hugonin, Msgr. Révérony, and even Msgr. Delatroëtte all became supporters and admirers of Thérèse even during her lifetime: the Bishop and the Vicar General, before her entrance into Carmel; and Msgr. Delatroëtte, a few years afterward.)

THE GOOD THAT THÉRÈSE RECEIVED FROM PRIESTS

Thérèse also received, I would say mostly received, much good from priests. About two months after her entrance into Carmel, Thérèse makes a general Confession to Fr. Almire Pichon, whom she also chose as her spiritual director. "At its termination," Thérèse would later write, "[Fr. Pichon] spoke the most consoling words I ever heard in my life." Fr. Pichon told Thérèse: "In the presence of God, the Blessed Virgin, and all the saints, I DECLARE THAT YOU HAVE NEVER COMMITTED A MORTAL SIN." And, he added: "My child, may Our Lord always be your superior and your novice master" (Ms A, 70r°).

Thérèse, recounting her first day in Carmel, recalls the reason why she had entered Carmel. "I had declared at the feet of Jesus-Victim, in the examination preceding my profession, what I had come to Carmel for: 'I came to save souls and especially to pray for priests'" (Ms A, 69v°). Let's take a brief look at this exchange of charity, between Thérèse and priests, after Thérèse's entrance into Carmel.

---

[13] *Letter* 261 (July 26th, 1897).

THÉRÈSE'S AND CÉLINE'S PRAYER FOR PRIESTS

Thérèse engaged in a thick correspondence with Céline, especially during the years of hardship and suffering due to their dear father Louis' sickness. (Louis Martin suffered, in fact, from cerebral arteriosclerosis from 1888 until his death in 1894.) Léonie and Céline even rented a small apartment near to the *Bon Sauveur* Hospital in Caen, where their father was recovered, for some months (February 19th to May 14th, 1889). Thérèse never ceased to encourage Céline, later calling her the "*ange visible*" (visible angel) next to their father (cf. LT 161). While encouraging Céline in her mission of charity toward their dear father Louis, Thérèse also encouraged her in her vocation, sharing her spiritual lights with her, and inviting her to participate in her mission to pray for priests. Shortly after Léonie and Céline had returned from Caen, in July of 1889, Thérèse wrote to Céline:

> Céline, during the SHORT MOMENTS [of this life] that *remain to us*, let us not lose our time... let us save souls... souls are being lost like flakes of snow, and Jesus weeps, and we... we are thinking of our sorrow without consoling our Fiancé... Oh, Céline, let us live for souls... let us be apostles... let us save especially the souls of priests; these souls should be more transparent than crystal... Alas, how many bad priests, priests who are not holy enough... Let us pray, let us suffer for them, and, on the last day, Jesus will be grateful. We shall give Him souls!...
>
> Céline, do you understand the cry of my soul? (LT 94).[14]

In the years 1889–1890, the "cry of her soul," to Céline, often repeats itself: "I feel that Jesus is asking *both of us* to quench *His thirst* by giving Him souls, the souls of *priests* especially" (LT 96).[15] "Céline, let us pray for priests, ah, pray for them. May our life be consecrated for them; Jesus makes me feel every day that He wills this from the both of us" (LT

---

[14] *Letter* 94 (July 14th, 1889).
[15] *Letter* 96 (October 15th, 1889).

108).[16] "Dear Céline, I *always* have the same thing to say to you. Ah! Let us pray for priests; each day shows how few the friends of Jesus are" (LT 122).[17]

AN IMPORTANT ENCOUNTER WITH FR. ALEXIS PROU

We must also remember the important encounter with Fr. Alexis Prou, Franciscan Recollect, who preached the Spiritual Exercises in October of 1891. Thérèse would later recount:

> I felt disposed to say nothing of my interior dispositions [to the priest] since I didn't know how to express them, but I had hardly entered the confessional when I felt my soul expand. After speaking only a few words, *I was understood* in a marvelous way and my soul was like a book in which this priest read better than I did myself. He launched me full sail upon the waves of *confidence and love* which so strongly attracted me, but upon which I dared not advance (Ms A, 80v°).

This encounter with Fr. Alexis Prou—even though Thérèse only spoke to him twice in her entire life, during that week of Spiritual Exercises—proved to be fundamental for the development and later "blossoming" of her "Little Way" of confidence and love.

THÉRÈSE'S POEMS: AN EXPRESSION OF HER CHARITY TOWARD PRIESTS

Thérèse mentions "priests" six times in her *Poems*.[18] In her *Poem* 1, *The Divine Dew, or the Virginal Milk of Mary*, she refers to Jesus as the "Eternal Priest, Sacerdotal Lamb" (cf. P 1). Whereas, in her last poem, *Poem* 54, *Why I Love You, O Mary!*, Thérèse compares the Blessed Virgin Mary to

---

[16] *Letter* 108 (July 18th, 1890).

[17] *Letter* 122 (October 14th, 1890).

[18] See the "Concordances" of Thérèse's writings: *Les mots de Sainte Thérèse de l'Enfant-Jésus et de la Sainte-Face: Concordance générale établie par Soeur Geneviève, o.p., de Clairefontaine Soeur Cécile, o.c.d., du Carmel de Lisieux, Jacques Lonchampt* (Lonrai (Orne): Les Éditions du Cerf, 1996, 657. (Voice: "*Prêtre.*")

a "priest at the altar." "Mary, at the top of Calvary standing beside the Cross/ To me you seem like a priest at the altar,/ Offering your beloved Jesus, the sweet Emmanuel" (P 54).

The other four recurrences in Thérèse's *Poems* of the term "*prêtre*" are to be found in four different poems, and they all refer to priests as ordained ministers. In her *Poem* 17, *Living on Love!*—which Céline would later define as "the King" of Thérèse's poetry[19]— Thérèse mentions the priest in stanza 10.

> Living on love, O my Divine Master,
> Is begging You to spread Your Fire
> In the holy, sacred souls of Your Priest.
> May he be purer than a seraphim in Heaven!...
> Ah! glorify Your Immortal Church!
> Jesus, do not be deaf to my sighs.
> I, her child, sacrifice myself for her,
> I live on Love (P 17).

The whole *Poem* 17, *Living on Love!*, has a Eucharistic theme to it. In fact, Thérèse composed the poem during the Forty Hours of Adoration before the opening of the Lenten season, 1895. At the end of the three days of Adoration, during the evening Recreation time, Thérèse committed to writing the poem that she had composed, in her heart, during the long hours in front of the Blessed Sacrament. A stanza on priests, thus, could not be lacking.

Thérèse composed most of her poetry upon request, as a gift of charity toward her nun-sisters. Her *Poem* 40, *The Sacristans of Carmel*, was no exception. In November of 1896, Sr. Marie-Philomène, who was in charge of the making of hosts for sale to outside buyers,[20] requested Thérèse to write

---

[19] See the Introduction to *Poem* 17, in *The Poetry of Saint Thérèse of Lisieux*, transl. Kinney, 89.

[20] According to the Carmel of Lisieux Archives website, the sale of hosts brought in nearly 1,600 francs a year in profit for the Lisieux monastery. The website states: "At the time of Thérèse, the Carmelite nuns supported themselves, from the work of their hands, the products of their garden and a few donations. They spent little: no heating, kerosene for lighting, [...] very simple food. The buildings were constructed from donations [...]. The livelihood of the sisters was essentially produced by: the production of

her a poem which could help to "animate," as it were, this everyday task. Thérèse readily agreed and composed *The Sacristans of Carmel*:

Here below our sweet office
Is to prepare for the altar
The bread and wine of the Sacrifice
Which brings "Heaven" to earth!
O supreme mystery, Heaven
Hides in humble bread,
For Heaven is Jesus Himself,
Coming to us each morning.
There are no queens on earth
Who are happier than we.
Our office is a prayer
Which unites us to our Spouse.
This world's greatest honors
Cannot compare
To the deep, celestial peace
Which Jesus lets us savor.
We bring a holy envy
For the work of our hands,
For the little white host
Which is to veil our divine Lamb.
But His love has chosen us.
He is our Spouse, our Friend.
We are also hosts
Which Jesus wants to change into Himself.
Sublime mission of the Priest,
You become our mission here below.
Transformed by the Divine Master,
It is He who guides our steps.
We must help the apostles
By our prayers, our love.

altar bread, [embroidery for priestly vestments], and painted images" (my translation). See https://archives.carmeldelisieux.fr/au-carmel-du-temps-de-therese/le-style-de-vie/le-travail/le-travail-des-ornements/ (accessed on February 25th, 2026). The quotation above speaks of "a few donations." Among the most important benefactors of the Lisieux Carmel was St. Louis Martin himself, who often brought fish—that he caught himself—and other foods to the Carmel to provide for his daughters and the other nuns in the monastery.

Their battlefields are ours.
For them we fight each day.
The hidden God of the tabernacle
Who also hides in our hearts,
O what a miracle! At our voice
Deigns to pardon sinners!
Our happiness and our glory
Is to work for Jesus.
His beautiful Heaven is the ciborium
We want to fill with souls!... (P 40).

"Their battlefields are ours." This phrase, for a priest like myself, is touching and comforting. To know that Thérèse, from Heaven, is praying for me, for us, is a source of strength, inspiration, consolation. And that others, perhaps like Thérèse, in the world today, are still doing the same.[21]

Now, Thérèse was well aware that her task of praying for priests was arduous; but she also knew that she was not alone. Turning to the Blessed Virgin Mary in her *Poem* 49, *To Our Lady of Perpetual Help*, she wrote: "When I'm struggling, O my dear Mother,/ You strengthen my heart in the fight,/ For you know, at the evening of this life/ I want to offer Priests to the Lord! . . ." (P 49).

THÉRÈSE'S TWO "BROTHERS" IN THE MISSIONS: FR. MAURICE BELLIÈRE AND FR. ADOLPHE ROULLAND

Thérèse had always desired to have brothers who would become missionary priests. When St. Zélie was pregnant with Thérèse, she had believed that Thérèse was a boy (because of the baby's extraordinary strength) and had wished that her child would become a missionary priest. God was faithful to their desires. Not in the way they had thought, but in an even better way.

Thérèse explains, at length, the way she was entrusted by her Prioress(es) with these two missionary brothers.

---

[21] My thoughts turn also to my dear Foundress, Mother Maria Elisabetta Patrizi, who died on July 12th 2020 (which also happens to be the Feast Day of St. Louis and Zélie Martin).

FR. MAURICE BELLIÈRE (LEFT) AND FR. ADOLPHE ROULLAND (RIGHT)

> It was our holy mother St. Teresa who sent me my first little brother as a feast day gift in 1895. I was in the laundry, very much occupied by my work, when Mother Agnes of Jesus took me aside and read a letter she had just received. It was from a young seminarian, inspired, he said, by St. Teresa of Ávila. He was asking for a sister who would devote herself especially to the salvation of his soul and aid him through her prayers and sacrifices when he was a missionary so that he could save many souls. He promised to remember the one who would become his sister at the Holy Sacrifice each day after he was ordained. Mother Agnes of Jesus told me she wanted me to become the sister of this future missionary (Ms C, 31v°).

Who was this "future missionary"? His name was Maurice Bellière; he was a maternal orphan. At that time, he was a seminarian for the diocese of Bayeux and aspiring missionary. He would actually leave for the missions on the very eve before Thérèse's death, that is September 29th, 1897. He entered the "*Pères Blancs*" (White Fathers) for his novitiate in Algeria (North Africa). He then became missionary in Malawi (Southeast Africa).[22]

---

[22] See Ste. Thérèse, *Manuscrits autobiographiques*, 404–5. Cf. note: "[Ms C,] 31v°, 14: *mon premier petit frère*."

While in Malawi, Fr. Bellière was unfortunately mistreated by his Superior, Msgr. Joseph Dupont. He became discouraged. In 1903, he caught black-water sickness (malaria), with subsequent kidney problems and sleeping sickness. He prepared himself for death. However, he was diagnosed in time and treated with the drugs available at the time. The malaria however, had affected his mental health. He may possibly have had, as well, a brain tumor. Two years later, in 1905, he "laid down his arms" as a missionary and returned to France without his Superiors' permission. Called to respond for his actions at the White Fathers' General Council, he was *not* severely punished but was told to return to Africa; his quickly deteriorating health, however, did not permit him to do so. Placed in a recovery house for sick missionaries in Belgium, he was dismissed by the doctor who suggested he return to the fresh air of Normandy. Five months later, his adoptive mother died. Most likely due to this sudden loss, Fr. Maurice's mental and physical health "plummeted." A priest-friend found him wandering around aimlessly in Normandy, and interned him in the psychiatric ward of the *Bon Sauveur* Hospital in Caen—the very same hospital in which St. Louis Martin, Thérèse's father, had been hospitalized from 1889 to 1892. Fr. Maurice Bellière died there on July 14th, 1907, at thirty-three years of age.[23]

Although Fr. Maurice's story has a tragic end, and Fr. Maurice himself considered his life a failure, it's not too difficult to see a greater plan. There are various signs of God's closeness to Fr. Maurice, as well as Thérèse's. The hardships of missionary life, the ill treatment of his Superior, his sickness—both physical and mental—and the apparent "failure" of his career; and even more evident, his interment in the *Bon Sauveur* Hospital and his death at thirty-three years of age. An attentive eye can pick out the "true side" of the tapestry, as St. Padre Pio would say: we see the side (that of our earthly life) with

---

[23] For this summary of mine on Fr. Maurice Bellière, see the article on him written by the White Fathers on their official website: https://www.peres-blancs.org/Pere_Maurice_Belliere.htm (accessed on February 25th, 2026).

all of the loose threads and all seems like a "mess." When we die, God turns over the tapestry and we see things as He does. Did not Jesus Himself suffer hardships during His public ministry of three years? Was He not also ill-treated by His "superiors," the chief priests and the scribes, as well as the Roman governor Pontius Pilate and the King of the Jews, Herod? Did not Jesus's "career" also end (on the cross) as an apparent failure (until His glorious Resurrection), at precisely thirty-three years of age? And the final touch: Fr. Maurice's internment in the *Bon Sauveur* Hospital, where St. Louis Martin had been interned for over three years. Indeed, God and St. Thérèse had not abandoned him. The abandonment was only apparent—to men's eyes.

Thérèse wrote eleven letters, in all, to Maurice Bellière. And he wrote twelve to her (including a holy card he sent her).[24] There's no time now to analyze them all. In Patrick Ahern's now renowned book, *Maurice and Thérèse: The Story of a Love*, one can reread and enjoy their correspondence. From her fourth letter onward, Thérèse would address him with "My dear little Brother." She wrote: "My dear little Brother, My pen, or rather my heart, refuses to call you 'Monsieur l'Abbé' from now on; and our good Mother has told me that in writing to you, I may use the name I always employ when I speak of you to Jesus" (LT 224). Needless to say, Thérèse soon set about teaching to Maurice her "Little Way" of confidence, trust, and abandonment to God.

Thérèse was entrusted, however, with two missionary brothers. It is worthwhile listening to Thérèse herself:

> It is time to resume the story of my brothers who now hold such a large place in my life. Last year at the end of the month of May, I remember how you called me one day before we went to the refectory. My heart was beating very fast when I entered your cell, dear Mother;

---

[24] Cf. Ste. Thérèse de l'Enfant-Jésus et de la Sainte-Face, *Édition critique des Œuvres Complètes, en huit volumes*, 2nd edn., "Nouvelle Édition du Centenaire," *Correspondance Générale*, vol. 2 (1890–1897) (Lonrai: Éditions du Cerf/Desclée De Brouwer, 1992), 1439–40.

> I was wondering what you could have to tell me since this was the very first time you called me in this way. After having told me to be seated, you asked me: "Will you take charge of the spiritual interests of a missionary who is to be ordained and leave very soon?" And then, Mother, you read this young priest's letter in order that I might know exactly what he was asking. My first sentiment was one of joy which was immediately replaced by fear. I explained, dear Mother, that having already offered my poor merits for one future apostle, I believed I could not do it for the intentions of another, and that, besides, there were many sisters better than I who would be able to answer his request. All my objections were useless. You told me that one could have several brothers. Then I asked you whether obedience could double my merits. You answered that it could, and you told me several things which made me see that I had to accept a new brother without any scruples. In the bottom of my heart, Mother, I was thinking the same way as you, and since *"the zeal of a Carmelite embraces the whole world,"* I hope with the grace of God to be useful to more than *two* missionaries and I could not forget to pray for all without casting aside simple priests whose mission at times is as difficult to carry out as that of apostles preaching to the infidels [...]. Well then! This is how I am spiritually united to the apostles whom Jesus has given me as brothers: all that I have, each of them has, and I know very well that God is too good to make divisions; He is so rich He can give without any measure everything I ask Him...(Ms C, 33r°–33v°).

Who then, was this second missionary "brother" of Thérèse? Fr. Adolphe Roulland (1870–1934). While Fr. Maurice Bellière had lived a life of apparent "unsuccess," at least on human terms, Fr. Adolphe Roulland instead lived a brilliant career as a missionary.

Adolphe Roulland was born near Bayeux (Normandy) in 1870. He was a good student and a hard worker. He apparently hesitated, after his classical studies, in following his vocation. We know this from a letter of Thérèse herself. On November 1st, 1896, Thérèse responded to a letter of his, stating:

> On September 8th, 1890, your missionary vocation was saved by Mary, Queen of Apostles and Martyrs; on that same day, a little Carmelite became the spouse of the King of Heaven. Saying an eternal farewell to the world, her sole aim was to save souls, especially the souls of apostles. She asked Jesus, her divine Spouse, particularly for an apostolic soul; unable to be a priest herself, she wanted a priest to receive the Lord's graces in her place, and that he might have the same aspirations and the same desires as she...(LT 201).

Adolphe had decided, thus, on September 8th, 1890—the same day of Thérèse's Profession—to enter the Seminary. He did so promptly, in October of the same year. Two years later, having completed his studies in Philosophy, he entered the Seminary of the Foreign Missions in Paris, France. Shortly before his priesthood ordination, he asked Fr. Norbert of the Premonstratensians of Mondaye to request the Prioress of the Lisieux Carmel, Mother Marie de Gonzague, if she could ask one of her nuns to pray for him in a special way and so ensure his apostolic fruitfulness. She immediately thought of Sr. Thérèse of the Child Jesus and proposed her, saying "She is the best among my good ones."[25]

Fr. Adolphe was ordained a priest on June 28th, 1896. Thérèse had the joy of meeting her new missionary brother in the Carmel of Lisieux parlor (albeit separated by the grate) on July 3rd, only a few days later. He celebrated Mass and then spoke with Thérèse. She had already sent him, as a gift for his first Mass on June 29th, a corporal, a purificator, and a pall which she herself painted for him (cf. LT 189).

---

[25] The source for this summary of Fr. Adolphe Roulland's biographical experience is the official website of the "Institute of Research France-Asia" founded and promoted by the "Foreign Missions of Paris" Congregation, of whom Fr. Adolphe Roulland was a member. I will be drawing from the "Obituary Letter" written by his same confreres shortly after his death. See https://irfa.paris/en/missionnaire/2226-roulland-adolphe/ (accessed on February 25th, 2026).

PALL TO BE PLACED ON THE CHALICE FOR MASS,
PAINTED BY THÉRÈSE FOR FR. ADOLPHE ROULLAND

Thérèse also placed a map of Sichuan, China, on the wall of her cell (her room) so as to better follow her missionary brother's movements, as described to her in his letters (cf. LT 193). There is no time now to analyze all of their letters, nor to recount all of the adventures lived by Fr. Roulland in China. Suffice it to say that he was later called to the Minor and then the Major Seminary in Sichuan to teach; and then became a parish priest, founding and constructing about 20 schools to better the population's life and education. He was then recalled to Paris in 1909 to serve as Director of the Seminary; he would later serve as Chaplain in a hospital and Master of Novices in his Congregation. He died peacefully in 1934, at 63 years of age.

Already in Thérèse's second letter to Fr. Adolphe, her *Letter* 193 (July 30th, 1896), she spoke to him on fraternal ("*Mon Frère*") and affectionate terms. Fully aware of her grave illness, she concluded her letter stating:

> Farewell [*A Dieu*], my Brother... distance can never separate our souls, and even death will make our union more intimate. If I go to Heaven soon, I will ask Jesus for permission to visit you in Sichuan, and we will continue our apostolate together. In the meantime, I will always be united with you through prayer, and I ask Our Lord to never let me feel joy while you are suffering. I would even wish for my Brother to always have the consolations while I have the trials; is that perhaps selfish?... No, because my only *weapon* is love and suffering, while your sword is that of the word and apostolic labors. Once again, farewell [*à Dieu*], my Brother; deign to bless the one whom Jesus has given you as a sister,
>
> Thérèse of the Child Jesus and
> of the Holy Face (LT 193)

SIXTH CHAPTER

St. Thérèse's charity toward her nun-sisters

INTRODUCTION: THÉRÈSE'S CONTACT WITH THE NUNS OF CARMEL *BEFORE* HER ENTRANCE

Before considering Thérèse's charity toward her nun-sisters while living in the Carmel of Lisieux, we must briefly take into account her contacts with these nuns before her entrance. As a matter of fact, Thérèse met several of the nuns before entering into Carmel, in the parlor of the monastery, while visiting her sister Pauline (Sr. Agnes of Jesus). The most significant encounter, and really the only one worth mentioning for now, was with the Prioress, Mother Marie de Gonzague. It was Pauline, of course, who introduced her to Thérèse.

Before speaking of the Prioress, however, we must spend a few words on Pauline. You will probably recall that, when their mother Zélie died—actually, on the day of her funeral—Thérèse had chosen Pauline as her "second mother." And, in reality, God had chosen Pauline as an instrument to guide Thérèse in her own vocation. Thérèse wrote: "I was very proud of my two sisters [Marie and Céline], but the one who was my *ideal* from childhood was Pauline. When I was beginning to talk, Mama would ask me: "What are you thinking about?" and I would answer invariably: "Pauline!" (Ms A, 6v°). Thérèse's attachment to Pauline, even as an infant, proved to be providential in God's plan for her. She wrote:

> I had often heard it said that surely Pauline would become a *religious*, and without knowing too much about what it meant I thought: "I too *will be a religious.*" This is one of my first memories and I haven't changed my resolution since then! It was through you, dear Mother, that Jesus chose to espouse me to Himself [...]. You were my *ideal*; I wanted to be like you, and

> it was your example that drew me toward the Spouse of Virgins at the age of two (Ms A, 6r°).

Pauline would later discern her vocation specifically to Carmel. Thérèse also felt called to Carmel. This could seem a childish imitation. However, Thérèse would later write in her childhood memories, addressed to Pauline:

> When thinking over all you had said, I felt that Carmel was the *desert* where God wanted me to go also to hide myself. I felt this with so much force that there wasn't the least doubt in my heart; it was not the dream of a child led astray but the *certitude* of a divine call; I wanted to go to Carmel not for *Pauline's sake* but for *Jesus alone*. I was thinking *very much* about things that words could not express but which left a great peace in my soul (Ms A, 26r°).

The day after having made these reflections, Thérèse confided them to Pauline. "She told me that soon I would go with her to see the mother prioress of the Carmel and that I must tell her what God was making me feel" (Ms A, 26r°). So, in the summer of 1882, they went to visit the Prioress together.

After Pauline's entrance (October 2nd, 1882), Thérèse went again to the parlor to visit with her sister and once again saw Mother Marie de Gonzague. A month or two later (November–December 1882), she wrote to the Prioress Mother Marie:

> Dear Mother,
>
> It has been a long time since I saw you, so I am very happy to write you to tell you about my little affairs. Pauline told me you were on retreat, and I'm coming to ask you to pray to little Jesus for me because I have many faults and want to correct them.
>
> I have to make my confession to you. For some time, I am always answering Marie back when she tells me to do something. It seems when Pauline was little and when she made excuses to Aunt at Le Mans, Aunt used to say to her: So many holes, so many pegs! But with me it's even worse. So I want to correct myself, and, into each little hole, put a pretty little flower which I'll offer to little Jesus to prepare myself for my First

> Communion. Won't you, dear Mother, pray for this? Oh! yes, this beautiful moment will come quickly, and how happy I shall be to have so many flowers to offer Him when the little Jesus comes into my heart.
>
> *Au revoir*, dear Mother. I kiss you tenderly; how I love you.
>
> Your little daughter, Thérésita (LT 9).

Thérèse's affection toward Mother Marie de Gonzague is evident in this *Letter* 9. She concludes her letter by writing "I kiss you tenderly; how I love you." Only two letters of Thérèse to the Prioress Mother Marie de Gonzague have been conserved, unfortunately. They are her *Letter* 9 and her *Letter* 190 (June 29th, 1896). Whereas, fifteen letters from the Prioress to Thérèse have been conserved, as well as nine holy cards or images that she gave or sent to Thérèse. (Mother Marie de Gonzague wrote seven letters and sent three holy cards to Thérèse before her entrance into Carmel.) The Prioress sometimes alludes to Thérèse's letters to her. Therefore, we know that Thérèse wrote to her, but her letters were unfortunately not conserved.[1] And so, Thérèse felt a special attraction and tie with the Prioress, as a spiritual mother, since her ninth year of age. The Prioress always encouraged her in her vocation to Carmel, and it was she—Mother Marie de Gonzague—who gave permission for Thérèse to enter at fifteen years of age, finally putting an end to the quarrels between the various superiors about her precocious entrance into Carmel. The bishop had placed the matter in the Prioress's hands, who declared herself favorable to Thérèse's youthful vocation.

THÉRÈSE'S "FIRST STEPS" IN RELIGIOUS LIFE

Thérèse wrote in her autobiographical memories:

> *Illusions*, God gave me the grace *not to have* A SINGLE ONE when entering Carmel. I found the religious life to be *exactly* as I had imagined it, no sacrifice astonished

[1] See Ste. Thérèse, *Correspondance générale*, vol. 2 (1890–1897), 1438–40.

> me and yet, as you know, dear Mother, my first steps met with more thorns that roses! Yes, suffering opened wide its arms to me and I threw myself into them with love (Ms A, 69v°).

Just what were these "thorns" that Thérèse encountered in her "first steps" in Carmel and in religious life? What was this suffering? Certainly—and most importantly—the worrisome health of her dear father, Louis, especially with his disappearance for four days in June of 1888, only a few months after her entrance into Carmel. But there were other smaller "thorns" as well. Thérèse defined them, in that time period, as "pinpricks." In her *Letter* 74, to Sr. Agnes of Jesus (Pauline), she wrote:

> Ask Jesus to make me generous during my retreat. He is riddling me with *pinpricks*; the poor little ball is exhausted. All over it has very little holes which make it suffer more than if it had only one large one! . . . Nothing near Jesus. Aridity! . . . Sleep! . . . But at least there is silence! . . . Silence does good to the soul . . . But creatures! Oh! creatures! . . . The little ball shudders from them! . . . Understand Jesus's little toy! . . . When it is the sweet Friend Who punctures His ball Himself, suffering is only sweetness, His hand is *so gentle*! . . . But creatures! . . . Those who surround me are very good, but there is something, I don't know what, that repels me! . . . I cannot give you any explanation. Understand your little soul. I am, however, VERY *happy*, happy to suffer what Jesus wants me to suffer. If He doesn't directly puncture His little ball, it is really He who directs the hand that punctures it! (LT 74).

These "pinpricks" are thus Jesus's action in her soul—but through the faults of her nun-sisters. Who was Thérèse referring to? We must remember that, out of the twenty-six nuns present at the time of Thérèse's entrance, only a handful were educated. Coarse and gruff personalities, mixed with daily fatigue and misunderstandings—added onto spiritual aridity—and family sufferings, were all wearing down on Thérèse. Again, who was Thérèse referring to? In her *Letter*

SR. SAINT VINCENT DE PAUL

76 to Sr. Agnes of Jesus, written the day after her *Letter* 74 (January 6th and 7th, 1889), Thérèse is explicit: "This morning I have endured some pain because of my Sister St. Vincent de Paul; I left with a very heavy heart." The Critical Edition of Thérèse's writings comments:

> Doubtless on the occasion of a fitting of alpargates (sandals of thick canvas, with cord soles) whose making was entrusted to Sr. Saint-Vincent de Paul. This latter, intelligent and original, hiding a heart of gold under gruff manners, never had sympathy for Thérèse, [who was] too slow and clumsy in practical works. She multiplied stinging remarks toward her, loud enough to be heard by the interested party. Thérèse contented herself with responding with a smile. After several years of these proceedings, Sr. Saint-Vincent de Paul loyally rendered homage to [Thérèse's] extraordinary virtue.[2]

TESTIMONIES OF THÉRÈSE'S NUN-SISTERS REGARDING HER FRATERNAL CHARITY

Those who have read *The Story of a Soul* know well how Thérèse interpreted and wrote about her own fraternal charity toward her nun-sisters, especially from her accounts in

---

[2] Cf. Ste. Thérèse, *Correspondance générale*, vol. 1 (1877–1890), 433, note a (translation mine).

Manuscript C. Fewer have heard or read the other nuns' testimonies. They are the true counter-proof that what Thérèse expressed in writing, in her *Manuscript* C, were not simply pious thoughts or meditations. They were real. In the sense that Thérèse not only wrote about them. She lived them. In first person.

To begin, I will quote Sr. Agnes of Jesus (Pauline), whose testimony was of course fundamental for the Processes of Beatification and Canonization of her sister Thérèse. For her Process of Beatification, Sr. Agnes of Jesus stated:

> In the course of [Thérèse's] religious life she often had to suffer from people's dislike of her, or from clashes of temperament or of mood, and, indeed, even from jealousy and spiteful behavior on the part of other nuns. Not only did she bear all this with patient equanimity, but she always tried to excuse their behavior. She also sought the company of such nuns in preference to that of others, and showed them the greatest kindness. I considered the conduct of one of these to be particularly reprehensible, but Sr. Thérèse insisted: "I assure you that I have the greatest compassion for Sr. X. If you knew her as well as I do, you would see that she is not responsible for all of the things that seem so awful to us. I remind myself that if I had an infirmity such as hers, and so defective a spirit, I would not do any better than she does, and then I would despair; she suffers terribly from her own shortcomings."[3]

These words of Thérèse, reported by her sister Pauline, faithfully echo Thérèse's spirit and way of thinking and viewing things. They recall her typical spiritual genius. Yet also her realism. A realism, however, always "gilded," as it were, with a positive attitude. Sr. Agnes' testimony continues in an even more surprising manner:

> [Thérèse] seemed to have a particular affection for those nuns who made her suffer, and she showed a preference for their company. Her eldest sister, Sr.

[3] O'Mahony, ed., *St. Thérèse of Lisieux by Those who Knew Her*, 50–51.

> Marie of the Sacred Heart [Marie Martin], often expressed her surprise at this, and was sometimes hurt by it. "I was a mother to her," she once complained, "and yet you'd think she loved that sister whom I can't stand better than she does me." At recreation she never went out of her way to meet her own three sisters. She chatted with any nun, no matter who she was, and especially with anyone she felt was lonely or left out. Though naturally very sensitive and affectionate, she was very reserved in external signs of affection and her manner imposed a certain respect. During her last illness someone was trying to kill the flies that were pestering her, when Sr. Thérèse made this rather surprising remark: "They are the only enemies I have, and since God has told us to love our enemies I am glad they give me this opportunity to do so. That is why I always spare them."[4]

Thérèse had truly understood and put to practice Jesus's recommendation: "But I tell you, love your enemies and pray for those who persecute you, that you may be children of your Father in heaven. He causes his sun to rise on the evil and the good, and sends rain on the righteous and the unrighteous" (Mt 5:44–45). Thérèse quotes the following Gospel passage, in fact, in an important letter of hers to Céline: "Be perfect, therefore, as your heavenly Father is perfect" (Mt 5:48; cf. LT 107).

Céline's testimony regarding Thérèse's love of neighbor, in the Process for her Beatification, is as surprising as that of Pauline's. It demonstrates the extraordinary strength of Thérèse, and her resolve to put her love for Jesus into practice. Céline testified:

> One day, just to encourage me in my efforts to overcome natural antipathy, [Thérèse] told me how much effort this cost herself. This was a real revelation to me, because she controlled herself so well that it looked effortless. I was still more surprised when she told

---

[4] Ibid., 51 (Sr. Agnes of Jesus's testimony; the passage cited is to be found in her response to the question regarding Thérèse's "love of neighbor").

> me the name of the sister who caused her these daily struggles with herself. Indeed, I found the Servant of God [Thérèse] so kind and considerate towards this sister that I would have taken her to be her best friend. It looked as if when someone was unpleasant to her, she became kinder, gentler, and more considerate towards that person in order to heal the embittered heart which she felt was suffering. She wanted me to follow her example in this, but I said: "It's too hard; I'll never be able to do it. I make good resolutions, and I see clearly what I have to do, but at the first encounter I give in." "If you are that easily overcome," she said, "it is because you do not soften your heart in advance. When you are exasperated with someone, the way to recover your peace of mind is to pray for that person and ask God to reward her for giving you an opportunity to suffer."[5]

These very concrete and creative pieces of advice that Thérèse would give to her sister and novice Céline (Sr. Genevieve of the Holy Face) are valid even today. "When you are exasperated with someone, the way to recover your peace of mind is to pray for that person and ask God to reward her for giving you an opportunity to suffer." A profound thought and an efficacious method, typical of Thérèse's spiritual genius! Another precious testimony of Céline's, from the same Process of Beatification, regards Thérèse's time as a novice. And the treatment she would habitually receive from the other nuns. Céline testified:

> From the time she [Thérèse] entered Carmel (1888) until the day I entered it myself (September 1894), finding myself separated from the Servant of God, I have no more personal observations to present. However, I saw her at the parlor every eight days, like my other Carmelite sisters. I learned in these interviews that my little sister had much to suffer in the novitiate. Above all, my sister Pauline (Mother Agnes of Jesus) would tell me her displeasure at seeing our little sister

[5] Ibid., 132 (Céline's testimony, quoted above, is part of her response to the question regarding Thérèse's virtue of charity toward her neighbor).

> badly cared for, exposed to the opposition of many and scolded for no reason. Thérèse then with an angelic air consoled her [Pauline], assured her that she was not unhappy and that she had everything she needed to live. I still see her [Thérèse], pale, but saintly joyful to suffer for the good Lord. From these conversations at the parlor it emerged that the main causes of these trials were, first, an almost uninterrupted state of dryness in prayer. Second: the indiscretion of some nuns who abused her heroic patience. Seeing her so sweet, without ever complaining, all the leftover food was passed on to this child, who should have been well fed instead. Several times she had on her plate nothing but a few heads of herring or some leftovers reheated for several days in a row. Third: the quite defective government of the community by Mother Marie de Gonzague, whose unstable and bizarre character made the nuns suffer greatly.[6]

These descriptions of Céline help us to understand an important fact: if we do not become saints, or at least strong in virtue, it is not the fault of those around us. It is our choice. The environment around us does *not* hinder our free will, and our personal and free choice to love, or not to love; to say "yes" to the Lord or to say "no" to Him, in the ordinary circumstances of everyday life. Thérèse chose to say "yes." And it was precisely the adverse environment that allowed her to grow, develop, and mature in her virtues—with the grace of God, of course.

Let us proceed listening, still, to a few other testimonies of Thérèse's nun-sisters. Sr. Marie of the Trinity, one of Thérèse's novices, provides some very telling and significant examples of Thérèse's fraternal charity. Although a bit long, I will report most of her testimony regarding Thérèse's "love of neighbor." It is truly worthwhile.

---

[6] Cf. *I Testimoni di Teresa di Gesù Bambino dai Processi di Beatificazione e Canonizzazione*, transl. Suor Amata Ruffinengo (Rome: Edizioni OCD, 2004), 115 (translation is mine). Céline, in the passage cited above, was responding to the question: "Novitiate. Profession. Attitude of the Ecclesiastical Superior. Behavior of the Servant of God in the time of her formation" (my translation).

Sr. Thérèse was very soft-hearted where other people's suffering was concerned, and she always showed it. She said to me: "Whenever I see one of the sisters suffering, and I have no permission to speak to her, I ask Jesus to comfort her Himself." She invited me to do likewise, and assured me that this was very pleasing to Jesus.

I have remarked more than once that when the community worked together she would place herself next to the sisters who seemed downcast or depressed. Since she could not speak to them [because of the Rule of silence], she smiled affectionately at them and tried to be as obliging as possible. There used to be a sister (she has since left us) who had moods of the blackest depression. Nobody could ever work with her for long. Sr. Thérèse took pity on this unhappy person and, seeing a great opportunity for sacrificing herself more fully for God's sake, she asked Mother Prioress to let her help this sister in her work. This heroic gesture brought her a great deal of suffering, but she bore it all with unfailing humility and gentleness.

For two or three months Sr. Thérèse was assistant portress to an elderly nun who, though a very good religious, had a temperament that would try the patience of a saint. She was also exasperatingly slow and very eccentric in her ways. One day I lost my patience with her, and she retorted that Sr. Thérèse never spoke to her like that. I told the Servant of God about this, and she said: "Be very gentle with her; she's not well. Besides, it's only charity to let her think she is rendering us a service, and it gives us an opportunity to practice patience. You are complaining after only a few words with her; what would you do if you had to listen to her all day, as I have to? Now, you can do what I do. It's really very easy. All you have to do is to mellow your soul with charitable thoughts; you then feel such peace that you no longer get irritated."

Another time she said: "It is perhaps at recreation more than anywhere else that one finds opportunities for sanctifying oneself by the practice of charity. If you want to profit by it, don't go there for your own recreation; concentrate on making it a recreation for

> others." And she literally practiced what she preached. I noticed that her only care was to please others, and she did it so naturally that you would think she did it for her own enjoyment.[7]

Thérèse's advice to Sr. Marie of the Trinity, her novice, to "mellow your soul with charitable thoughts" may seem like some sort of psychological "trick." In reality—probably without her realizing it—Thérèse inserted herself here into the huge Eastern Christian tradition, starting with Origen, through to the Desert Fathers, up to the Byzantine, Greek, and Russian traditions of spirituality. I'm referring to the doctrine of "spiritual combat" and to the spiritual exertion of keeping out *loghismoi* (evil thoughts) insinuated by the demons. The power of *thoughts* was something that the Eastern Fathers were very well aware of. (Thérèse actually did read and hear something of the Desert Fathers and Desert Mothers, by the way.)

It is still worthwhile to quote two other testimonies. Regarding those very sisters (among others) who mistreated Thérèse. Their testimony is the ultimate counter-proof of Thérèse's heroic—yet delicate—fraternal charity. The first we will turn to is that of Sr. Martha of Jesus, one of her novices. Désirée Cauvin—her secular name—was an orphan who had grown up in various orphanages. She was emotionally unbalanced. All the nuns feared her violent temper and angry outbursts. At the same time, she was a "generous and tireless worker, and tried hard, with Thérèse's help, to overcome her temper."[8] Sr. Martha of Jesus testified, regarding Thérèse's "love of neighbor":

> In her great charity she always found an excuse for those who hurt her, by looking at their intentions, and always took care to be very nice to them. One day I asked her: "How come you always smile so sweetly

[7] O'Mahony, ed., *St. Thérèse of Lisieux by Those who Knew Her*, 238–39 (Sr. Marie of the Trinity's testimony, cited above, is part of her response to the question regarding Thérèse's "love of neighbor").

[8] See the *Introduction* to Sr. Martha of Jesus's testimony on Thérèse in ibid., 216.

when Sr. X speaks to you? It cannot be because of any attraction because she is always making you suffer." She answered: "That is precisely why I love her, and why I show her so much affection; how could I prove I loved Jesus if I behaved otherwise toward those who hurt me?" [...]

I must bear special testimony to the Servant of God's dealings with myself. She was kindness and charity itself to me; only in Heaven will it be realized how much she did for me, and the lengths to which she carried her self-sacrifice on my behalf. I inflicted a great deal of suffering on her through my difficult temperament. But I can honestly say that she always remained calm and kind. I would even go so far as to say that the more I made her suffer, the more she seemed to show me preference and kindness. She never rejected me, in spite of the frequency of my visits; I never noticed even the slightest annoyance in the way she received me. Through her admirable virtues I came to love her dearly. Still, I was sometimes a bit jealous, and would get angry when she called attention to my shortcomings. On such occasions I used to go away and refuse to speak to her. But such was her charity that she always sought me out to try and help me, and her gentleness never failed to win me over.

One day I was upset and said some very hurtful things to her. She just went on talking calmly and gently, asking me to help her with some work she had to do. I gave in, still muttering to myself at the inconvenience she was causing me. Then I thought I would see how far her patience could be stretched, so, to try her virtue, I decided not to answer when she spoke to me. But I failed to upset her, and ended up asking her to forgive me for being so rude. Sr. Thérèse did not scold me, nor did she say a word to hurt me; she just encouraged me to be more obliging in future, and taught me the error of my ways. Her charity towards me never ceases to amaze me, and I have often wondered what could make her so interested in a poor lay-sister. I can find no words adequate to express the self-sacrifice with which she attended to my spiritual welfare.[9]

[9] Ibid., 219–20.

To complete this small sort of "painting" of Thérèse's fraternal charity toward her nun-sisters, we must listen to one more testimony—that of the very same sister who annoyed Thérèse so much: Sr. Thérèse of Saint-Augustine. In her *Preparatory Notes for the Ordinary Process*, she wrote:

> In community life, the Servant of God [Sr. Thérése of the Child Jesus] practiced the most exquisite charity, constantly forgetting herself for the happiness of the sisters, bearing without complaint—and without anyone being able to notice—the sufferings caused by the ill-will and jealousy of a few sisters who did not know how to recognize her virtue. She remained always patient, gentle, and amiable with them, welcoming them with a gracious smile, avoiding anything that could cause them pain, trying to be pleasing to them, and incessantly making excuses for them. Whenever she encountered a sister for whom her nature felt a certain distance or dislike, she would pray for her and offer to the good God the virtues she noticed in her.
>
> Sr. Thérèse of the Child Jesus was eager to render the services requested of her because she remembered the word of Our Lord: "Whatever you do to the least of mine, you do unto Me" [Mt 25:40]. When she was unable to do so, she excused herself so graciously that one could not help but show her gratitude anyway. She thus spent herself under the gaze of God without demanding anything in return. Certain characters took excessive advantage of her kindness, but she did not avoid them, because she held the maxim that one must never distance oneself from those who easily ask for favors. She showed the heroism of her charity toward a lay sister whom she assisted in her infirmity and who often showed her gratitude only through brusqueness; yet the Servant of God never grew weary of continuing her kind services. She was ingenious in finding ways to show her compassion to sisters she knew were suffering or afflicted. With a ravishing delicacy, she would say a word, or content herself with a smile if she could do no more. But this sympathy went straight to the heart; one knew it was true. Around her, an

> atmosphere of peace truly reigned—one felt as if in the presence of an angel![10]

Sr. Thérèse of St. Augustine wrote this powerful testimony—as did the other nuns—to better prepare herself for the official testimony of the Diocesan (Ordinary) Phase of Thérèse's cause. She wrote of "a sister for whom her [Sr. Thérèse of the Child Jesus's] nature felt a certain distance or dislike." That sister was her very self! Never—until the day she died (July 21st, 1929)—did Sr. Thérèse of St. Augustine discover the fact that she was the very same sister who had given so much annoyance to St. Thérèse![11] Her official testimony, given at the Ordinary Process for Thérèse's Beatification, was similar to her *Preparatory Notes*.

> The charity of Sr. Thérèse of the Child Jesus extended to all the sisters; there was no partiality in her way of acting. She gave affection and devotion to everyone, serving each one to the best of her ability with perfect self-abnegation. She was always amiable, even toward those who lacked delicacy in their conduct toward her. She welcomed them with the same smile, seeking to please them and avoiding anything that could be an occasion for pain or struggle for them. Having entered the Carmel at the age of fifteen and finding herself there with her own [biological] sisters, one might have thought she would seek from them the consolations and joys of family; this was not the case; she wanted her sacrifice to be complete in everything. Thus, she never showed more preference to her sisters according to nature than to those united to her by the bonds of religion. During one of the "licenses" [recreation periods] in which we have permission to speak,

[10] See the Carmel of Lisieux Archives website, at https://archives.carmeldelisieux.fr/au-carmel-du-temps-de-therese/la-communaute/soeur-therese-de-st-augustin/notes-preparatoires-de-sr-therese-de-st-augustin/ (the translation is mine; accessed on February 25th, 2026).

[11] The circular or obituary letter dedicated to Sr. Thérèse of St. Augustine, written by the Mother Prioress Agnes of Jesus (Pauline Martin), shortly after her death, hints to this fact. See https://archives.carmeldelisieux.fr/au-carmel-du-temps-de-therese/la-communaute/soeur-therese-de-st-augustin/circulaire-de-soeur-therese-de-st-augustin/ (accessed on February 25th, 2026).

> I made this remark to her: "I am not asking you to come with us for a moment; having your sisters here, you must have very little free time."—"Oh! do not believe that," she answered me, "I do not give them more time than to the others; you are all my sisters."[12]

Sr. Thérèse of St. Augustine, therefore, highly praised the virtue of Thérèse. But the most telling proof of Thérèse's charity is the fact that her "annoying" fellow sister never realized that it was precisely she who had so tried the saint's patience! Many years later—in the last years of her life—Sr. Thérèse of St. Augustine spoke about her own youthful defects, in her mannerisms and ways of being. She said:

> I was working seriously to correct my faults; however, my efforts were not crowned with success. The most prominent one—the stiffness of my words and manners—continued to be frequently held against me, to the point that I almost despaired of overcoming myself, since my good will could not succeed... I was also very prone to impatience: if I asked for a favor, it had to be done for me immediately; I did not know how to wait. And above all, I loved to feed my self-love: I remember that, having made a vow of abandonment to God's good pleasure, I did not want to speak of it to anyone, so as not to give others the idea of doing the same, in order to reserve for myself some superiority in perfection. Oh! How I blush at this baseness, at my narrow-mindedness, and at my selfishness back then![13]

Her rude and stiff manners were apparently very trying for Thérèse's sensitive and refined nature. And yet, Thérèse found a creative and positive way of "getting around" her own feelings. She thought to herself, as she would later write, "And

---

[12] See https://archives.carmeldelisieux.fr/naissance-dune-sainte/les-proces-la-sainte-de-therese/le-proces-ordinaire/les-temoignages-du-proces-ordinaire/ (my translation, accessed on February 25th, 2026).

[13] See the circular obituary letter written by Mother Agnes of Jesus: https://archives.carmeldelisieux.fr/au-carmel-du-temps-de-therese/la-communaute/soeur-therese-de-st-augustin/circulaire-de-soeur-therese-de-st-augustin/ (translation mine, accessed on February 25th, 2026).

still, she is a holy religious who must be very pleasing to God [... and] Jesus, the artist of souls, is happy when we don't stop at the exterior, but, penetrating into the inner sanctuary where He chooses to dwell, we admire its beauty." Thérèse gave her the "benefit of the doubt." And, in reality, she was not far off. Sr. Thérèse of St. Augustine made her Profession in the year 1877 (eleven years before St. Thérèse entered the monastery). Shortly thereafter, Sr. Thérèse of St. Augustine resolved to improve her difficult character. Mother Agnes of Jesus (Pauline) would write about this fact years later, in the obituary circular following her death.

> Finally, after many ups and downs, grace triumphed. One morning, spontaneously, this prayer escaped from [Sr. Thérèse of St. Augustine's] heart: "My God, make me suffer whatever You will, provided that I reach an intimate union with You. Listen neither to my complaints nor to my tears, but cut away everything that might hold me back from You; and even if I should ask You to stop, do not do it: it would be my nature speaking, but not my will." And never, thereafter, despite very painful trials, did she contradict her heroic prayer.[14]

Thérèse was confident that God was at work in the souls of her nun-sisters, and thus she always gave them the "benefit of the doubt," as she did even in the case of the nun she found most annoying, Sr. Thérèse of St. Augustine. And she was right in doing so. She commented, wisely, to her sister Céline one day, as they were walking in the garden of the monastery together, pointing to one of the fruit trees:

> Those pears aren't a bit attractive at present, are they? In the fall, however, when they are stewed and served to us in the refectory, we shall find them to our taste, and it will be hard to connect them with the fruit which we are looking at now. That is a good reminder of the truth that on the Last Day, when we shall all be delivered from our faults and imperfections, those

---

[14] Ibid.

sisters, whose natural qualities may now be displeasing to us, might appear to us as great saints. And we shall perhaps gaze on them open-mouthed in wonder.[15]

THÉRÈSE'S OWN UNDERSTANDING AND INTERPRETATION OF HER FRATERNAL CHARITY TOWARD HER NUN-SISTERS

At this point, only one reflection remains. How did Thérèse interpret her own fraternal charity? Although an important question, we will seek out the answer only briefly, leaving the word to Thérèse herself. In her *Manuscript* C—written in the last months of her life—Thérèse wrote:

> Mother, when reading what I have just written, you could believe that the practice of charity is not difficult for me. It is true; for several months now I no longer have to struggle to practice this beautiful virtue. I don't mean by this that I no longer have any faults; ah! I am too imperfect for that. But I mean that I don't have any trouble in rising when I have fallen because in a certain combat I won a great victory; and the heavenly militia now comes to my aid since it cannot bear seeing me defeated after having seen me victorious in the glorious battle I am going to try to describe.
>
> There is in the community a sister who has the faculty of displeasing me in everything, in her ways, her words, her character, everything seems *very disagreeable* to me. And still, she is a holy religious who must be very pleasing to God. Not wishing to give in to the natural antipathy I was experiencing, I told myself that charity must not consist in feelings but in works; then I set myself to doing for this sister what I would do for the person I loved the most. Each time I met her I prayed to God for her, offering Him all her virtues and merits. I felt this was pleasing to Jesus, for there is no artist who doesn't love to receive praise for his works, and Jesus, the artist of souls, is happy when we don't stop at the exterior, but, penetrating into the inner sanctuary where He chooses to dwell,

[15] Sr. Geneviève of the Holy Face, *My Sister Saint Thérèse (CSG)*, authorized transl. by the Carmelite Sisters of New York of *Conseils et Souvenirs* (Rockford, Illinois: TAN Books and Publishers, 1992), 139.

> we admire its beauty. I wasn't content simply with praying very much for this sister who gave me so many struggles, but I took care to render her all the services possible, and when I was tempted to answer her back in a disagreeable manner, I was content with giving her my most friendly smile, and with changing the subject of the conversation, for the *Imitation* says: "*It is better to leave each one in his own opinion than to enter into arguments.*"
>
> Frequently, when I was at recreation (I mean during the work periods) and had occasion to work with this sister, I used to run away like a deserter whenever my struggles became too violent. As she was absolutely unaware of my feelings for her, never did she suspect the motives for my conduct and she remained convinced that her character was very pleasing to me. One day at recreation she asked in almost these words: "Would you tell me, Sr. Thérèse of the Child Jesus, what attracts you so much toward me; every time you look at me, I see you smile?" Ah! what attracted me was Jesus hidden in the depths of her soul; Jesus who makes sweet what is most bitter. I answered that I was smiling because I was happy to see her (it is understood that I did not add that this was from a spiritual standpoint) (Ms C, 13v°–14r°).

Thérèse had understood—as she wrote only a few pages earlier—that "charity must not remain hidden in the bottom of the heart" and that, as she wrote, "my love was not to be expressed only in words, for '*It is not those who say: "Lord, Lord!" who will enter the kingdom of heaven, but those who do the will of my Father in heaven*'" (cf. Ms C, 11v°–12r°). So Thérèse made sure to overcome her natural feelings and to demonstrate explicitly and in concrete ways—for example, with her best smile—her love for Jesus through her charity toward her nun-sisters.

It's important to remember, as well, that almost all of Thérèse's writings were done either through obedience—for example, her *Manuscripts* A and C—or because of a request on behalf of one of her nun-sisters, or as a gift for one or another of her Sisters, for their feast days or name days or Profession days, etc. This applies especially for Thérèse's *Poems* (almost all of them), but also for her *Plays*, written to cheer and give joy to her nun-sisters at Recreation and for special feast days. The same could be said, as well, of various of Thérèse's *Prayers*, written to help or to please one or another of her Sisters.

There's no time now to analyze all of Thérèse's *Poems*, nor her *Plays* or *Prayers*. We'll have to content ourselves with Thérèse's words in her *Manuscript* C which, in some way, reassume and synthesize her whole experience and teaching on fraternal charity, especially as regards her nun-sisters. She wrote: "Yes, I feel it, when I am charitable, it is Jesus alone who is acting in me, and the more united I am to Him, the more also do I love my sisters" (Ms C, 12v°).

SEVENTH CHAPTER

St. Thérèse's charity toward holy souls in Purgatory and in Heaven

INTRODUCTION: KNOWLEDGE AND LOVE

"No one can love at all a thing of which he is wholly ignorant," St. Augustine affirms in book 10, chapter 1 of his famous treatise on the Most Holy Trinity, *De Trinitate*. In other words, you cannot love something that you do not know. This is a universal truth, that regards, of course, the Most Holy Trinity; but it also regards all truths of faith and, in reality, all knowledge and all love. How could one love something or someone that he has absolutely no idea about and has never heard about?

Thérèse would come to know and love intimately the riches of Christian and Catholic doctrine; but above all, she came to know and love God Himself; Mary, the Mother of God; the angels and the saints; and all men and women of all time, for love of God. She would come to know and love God so much, that she would later become a Doctor of the Church!

In the current chapter, I'd like to "zoom in," as it were, on just one or two (extremely important) fragments of the entirety of Christian doctrine: holy souls in Purgatory and in Heaven; or rather, Thérèse's fraternal charity, or love, toward those souls. I was saying that Thérèse would come to know of and love this truth, and these persons, with the passage of time. When is it, then, that Thérèse first learned about the reality of holy souls living in Purgatory and in Heaven? And how did she learn of it? To love these souls, she must first have learned of them, for, again, "No one can love at all a thing of which he is wholly ignorant."

THE "ROOTS" OF THÉRÈSE'S KNOWLEDGE OF SUPERNATURAL TRUTHS: THE MARTIN FAMILY

Thérèse herself provides an answer to these questions in her childhood memoirs. She quotes a letter that her mother Zélie wrote to her sister Pauline on December 5th, 1875. Thérèse, at that point, was about a month away from turning three years old. Her mother Zélie had written:

> Baby [Thérèse] is a little imp; she'll kiss me and at the same time wish me to die. "Oh, how I wish you would die, dear little Mother!" When I scold her she answers: "It is because I want you to go to Heaven, and you say we must die to get there!" She wishes the same for her father in her outbursts of affection for him (Ms A, 4v°).

This is the first mention of "Heaven" that Thérèse reports, regarding her own words at an early age, in her writings. Shortly after, she recounts another episode from her infancy. She quotes once more from a letter written by her mother Zélie, again to Pauline, on October 29th, 1876. Thérèse was, at that point, about three years and eleven months old. Her mother Zélie wrote:

> Little Thérèse asked me the other day if she would go to Heaven. I told her "Yes" if she were good. She answered: "Yes, but if I'm not good, I'll go to hell. But I know what I will do. I will fly to you in Heaven, and what will God be able to do to take me away? You will be holding me so tightly in your arms!" I could see in her eyes that she was really convinced that God could do nothing to her if she were in her mother's arms (Ms A, 5v°).

This is the second time that Thérèse mentions "Heaven"—again, referring to herself as a baby—in her writings. Her candid innocence, as a three-year-old, is striking. Of course, she had not yet matured in her conception of who God really is, as she would years later. It is precisely her image of God, in fact, that she would acquire with the passage of time and with God's grace, that makes her such a spiritual genius and a Doctor of the Church. She would later write—just to make an example—a sublime intuition regarding God: "God is more tender than a mother" (Ms A, 80v°). Thérèse was turning twenty-three years old when she wrote this phrase. It's interesting to see this change of paradigm in Thérèse's conception of God, from her third to her twenty-third year. There is no need to hide from God's punishing eyes and arm, seeking refuge in a mother's protective arms, as she had ingenuously thought when she was three years old, because, after all, "God is more tender than a mother." In twenty years (from three to twenty-three years of age), God had infused in Thérèse—through grace, through her meditation of the Scripture, and many other events—a precise and moving knowledge and love of who He really is. "God is more tender than a mother." Thérèse would later write, to Fr. Roulland,

> I know one must be very pure to appear before the God of all Holiness, but I know, too, that the Lord is infinitely just; and it is this justice which frightens so many souls that is the object of my joy and confidence. To be just is not only to exercise severity in order to punish the guilty; it is also to recognize right intentions and to reward virtue. I expect as much from God's justice as from His mercy. It is because He is just that "He is compassionate and filled with gentleness, slow to punish, and abundant in mercy, for He knows our frailty, He remembers we are only dust. As a father has tenderness for his children, so the Lord has compassion on us!!" [...] (LT 226).

Thérèse, again—as we can see from this passage of her *Letter* 226 to Fr. Roulland—had matured her conception of God. The Holy Spirit, true Author of the Holy Scriptures, had opened and enlightened Thérèse's mind and soul in a special way. Thérèse penetrated into the Scriptures in a special and original way, as we can see from this quotation, in her *Letter* 226, of Psalm 102. She wrote this letter in May of 1897, about five months before her death. At its conclusion, she wrote: "This is, Brother, what I think of God's justice; my way is all confidence and love. I do not understand souls who fear a Friend so tender."

THÉRÈSE'S CONCEPTION OF HEAVEN, FORMED IN THE MARTIN FAMILY

Let's turn back, now, to Thérèse's conception of Heaven; we'll quickly move on, then, to her charity toward souls in Purgatory and in Heaven. Thérèse had learned of Heaven from her mother Zélie. "It is because I want you to go to Heaven, and you say we must die to get there!" she had said to her mother at only two years of age. So, it was thus in her family—from her parents and siblings—that Thérèse learned the first notions about Christian and Catholic faith. Her father Louis, in fact, would often speak of Heaven, sighing and singing about it: *"La Patrie! La Patrie!"* "The Homeland! The Homeland!" (This term became dear to Thérèse: she uses it 98 times in her writings, with almost exclusive reference to Heaven, not to the homeland of her nation, France.) The last words that Louis, her dear father, would speak in her presence were uttered by him in his last visit to the Carmel parlor. He had recently been discharged from the psychiatric ward, after 39 long months of recovery, in the *Bon Sauveur* hospital in Caen. Overcome by emotion and by his illness, Louis Martin was able to speak only two words: with his finger pointed upwards, he gave his last farewell to his beloved daughters in Carmel: *"Au ciel!"* ("See you in Heaven!").

THÉRÈSE'S CRY FOR HELP, TURNED TOWARD HEAVEN

Thérèse had been formed by her family to have an acute awareness of Heaven, and of the souls in Heaven. In fact, when Thérèse was only a teenager (thirteen years old), she turned to her four deceased siblings, asking them for help. She would later write:

> When Marie entered Carmel, I was still very scrupulous. No longer able to confide in her I turned toward Heaven. I addressed myself to the four angels who had preceded me there, for I thought that these innocent souls, having never known troubles or fear, would have pity on their poor little sister who was suffering on earth. I spoke to them with the simplicity of a child, pointing out that

> being the youngest of the family, I was always the most loved, the most covered with my sisters' tender cares, that if they had remained on earth they, too, would have given me proof of their affection. Their departure for Heaven did not appear to me as a reason for forgetting me; on the contrary, finding themselves in a position to draw from the divine treasures, they had to take *peace* for me from these treasures and thus show me that in Heaven they still knew how to love! The answer was not long in coming, for soon peace came to inundate my soul with its delightful waves, and I knew then that if I was loved on earth, I was also loved in Heaven. Since that moment, my devotion for my little brothers and sisters has grown and I love to hold dialogues with them frequently, to speak with them about the sadness of our exile, about my desire to join them soon in the fatherland [*la patrie*] (Ms A, 44r°)!

THÉRÈSE AND THE SAINTS IN HEAVEN

Thérèse recounts here how she experienced, already as a thirteen-year-old, the great love and healing help and intercession of her deceased siblings, in Heaven. Again, Thérèse had been opened to the truths of Heaven and about saints in Heaven since her early childhood. We know that very early on—around her fifth year of age—during Mass on Sundays, her father would invite her to listen attentively to the homilies: "When the preacher spoke about St. Teresa [of Ávila], Papa leaned over and whispered: 'Listen carefully, little queen, he's talking about your Patroness'" (Ms A, 17v°). It was also during Thérèse's readings, as a child, of various books about the French heroines, especially St. Joan of Arc, that Thérèse received a grace which, she wrote, "I have always looked upon as one of the greatest in my life [...]. I considered that I was born for *glory* [...]. He [God] made me understand my own *glory* would not be evident to the eyes of mortals, that it would consist in becoming a great *saint!*" (Ms A, 32r°). Thus, it was in meditating upon the lives of saints, as a child, that Thérèse was inspired, by God, to desire to become, she herself, a great saint.

Thérèse had a great veneration and a great love for saints;[1] on her pilgrimage to Rome—and all along the way—whenever she would visit the relics or some holy places in which saints had lived, she would touch her crucifix to the relics; or otherwise, she herself would try to get as near as possible and to touch, herself, these relics. She wrote: "Céline and I were very brave; we were always the first and were following the bishop closely in order to see everything pertaining to the relics of the saints and hear the explanation given by the guides" (Ms A, 58v°). She continued, writing about her pilgrimage to Italy:

> At Florence, I was happy to contemplate St. Magdalene de' Pazzi in the Carmelite choir. They opened the big grille for us. As we did not know we would enjoy this privilege and many wanted to touch their rosaries to the saint's tomb, I was the only one who could put my hand through the grating which separated us from the tomb. And so everybody was carrying rosaries to me and I was very proud of my office. I always had to find a way of *touching everything* (Ms A, 66r°).

THÉRÈSE'S CHARITY TOWARD HOLY SOULS IN PURGATORY AND TOWARD THE SAINTS IN HEAVEN, AFTER HER ENTRANCE INTO THE LISIEUX CARMEL

Let's take a jump forward now, in time. We must examine more closely Thérèse's charity, as a nun, toward holy souls in

---

[1] An excellent booklet which examines Thérèse from another point of view is the following: M. E. Patrizi, *Il Patto segreto. L'amicizia mistica di san Massimiliano Kolbe e santa Teresa di Lisieux* (Rome: C.d.C. Editrice, 2008). This study—written in Italian—analyzes the spiritual friendship between St. Maximilian Kolbe and St. Thérèse. Kolbe read Thérèse's autobiography, *The Story of a Soul*, in the years 1918–1919 while studying as a seminarian in Rome. (Thérèse had died in 1897.) From then on, Kolbe's spiritual friendship with Thérèse was destined only to grow . . . Considering that Kolbe's spirituality is largely based on the dogma of the Immaculate Conception, Thérèse's relationship with Mary is also addressed in the aforementioned study. On the same topic, see also the article: M. E. Patrizi, "P. Kolbe e la spiritualità di Santa Teresa di Gesù Bambino," *Rivista di Vita Spirituale* 53 (1999), 188–209. For ulterior insights and intuitions regarding Thérèse's relationship with Mary and her vocation to be "love in the heart of the Church," see two articles of the same author: "'La mia vocazione è l'amore.' Sulla scia di Maria," *Rivista di Vita Spirituale* 6 (1997), 753–62; "S. Teresa di Lisieux: 'Nella Chiesa io sarò l'amore,'" *La Madonna delle Laste* 11 (1996), 11.

Purgatory and in Heaven. About nine months after Thérèse's entrance into the Lisieux Carmel, she wrote a note to Pauline in which, for the first time, she explicitly mentions souls in Purgatory. I'm referring to Thérèse's *Letter* 74. In speaking about her upcoming Clothing Ceremony, when she was to enter Novitiate, she wrote: "On the day of my espousals [= Clothing Ceremony], I would like to convert *all* the sinners of this earth and to save all the souls in Purgatory!" (LT 74).

The idea of saving all the souls in Purgatory was dear to Thérèse particularly in moments that she held as being important and solemn. Coming near to her Clothing Ceremony, in her *Letter* 74, Thérèse expressed the desire to save all the souls in Purgatory. When preparing for her Profession (September 8th, 1890), Thérèse expressed the same desire. In her *Profession Note*, she wrote: "Jesus, allow me to save very many souls; let no soul be damned today; let all the souls in Purgatory be saved . . . Jesus, pardon me if I say anything I should not say. I only want to give You joy and to console You." In another of her *Prayers*, her most solemn and important prayer of all, her *Prayer* 6, *Act of Oblation to Merciful Love*, Thérèse wrote (between June 9th and 11th, 1895): "O My God! Most Blessed Trinity, I desire to *Love* You and make You Loved, to work for the glory of Holy Church by saving souls on earth and liberating those suffering in Purgatory." Thérèse's *regard*, her vision, her perception of reality and of the Church—in all three states, that is, militant, purgative, and triumphant—was growing and maturing. Thérèse wanted to save souls not only on earth, but also in Purgatory.

AN ALL-EMBRACING LOVE, UNTIL THE END

Considering Thérèse's charity toward souls in Purgatory, Céline would later testify, in the Beatification Process for her sister Thérèse:

> Her charity reached out, too, to the souls in Purgatory. She had made her "heroic offering" and entrusted all her daily merits to Our Lady so that she might use

> them for the benefit of those suffering souls; she had made the same arrangement regarding any prayers that would be offered for herself after her death.[2]

A year after her "heroic offering," that is, her *Act of Oblation to Merciful Love*, done in June of 1895, Thérèse had an important and consoling dream. She dreamt of Venerable Anne of Jesus, who—from Heaven, in her dream—had come to console her. She concluded her account of this dream with the words: "When I understood to what a degree *she* [Venerable Anne of Jesus] *loved me*, how *indifferent* I had been toward her, my heart was filled with love and gratitude, not only for the saint who had visited me but for all the blessed inhabitants of Heaven" (Ms B, 2v°).

After Thérèse's heroic offering, and her trial of faith—which was a trial of faith in the existence of Heaven—she herself entered through the doors of Paradise, on September 30th, 1897. Recounting, in her *Yellow Notebook*, the day of Thérèse's death, Pauline wrote:

> Suddenly, after having pronounced these [last] words, she [Thérèse] fell back, her head leaning to the right. Mother Prioress had the infirmary bell rung very quickly to call back the community.
>
> "Open all the doors," she said at the same time. These words had something solemn about them, and made me think that in Heaven God was saying them also to His angels (CJ, September 30th).

[2] O'Mahony, ed., *St. Thérèse of Lisieux by Those who Knew Her*, 130.

EIGHTH CHAPTER
St. Thérèse's charity toward her spiritual sons and daughters

INTRODUCTION: THÉRÈSE'S "*MATERNAL*" CHARITY

In this chapter, we'll be changing our perspective slightly. If, so far, we've been concentrating on Thérèse's *fraternal* charity, which is the specific object of this study, let us now examine her fraternal charity toward her spiritual sons and daughters. In other words, Thérèse often expressed her fraternal charity as maternal charity. This is especially true as regards certain categories of persons: in particular, sinners, souls in Purgatory, and even some of her nun-sisters. Yet, the same holds true, at least in part, for priests and even toward some of her family members, such as her sisters Léonie and Céline and her cousins Marie and Jeanne Guérin. Paradoxically, toward the end of her life, sometimes Thérèse reverses roles even with her godmother and eldest sister Marie, with her "second mother" Pauline and with her Mother Prioress, Mother Marie de Gonzague, and—at least in a few occasions—from "daughter" becomes a "mother" and a "teacher." We'll see in the last chapter that, although Thérèse's charity toward all men and all women of all time is better "categorized" as being a "fraternal charity"—a true sister for all,—at the same time, this does not exclude her from being a "spiritual mother" toward all men and women of all time, inasmuch as her charity participates in that of God's.

THE "FOUR CHORDS" OF THE HUMAN HEART

Fr. François-Marie Léthel, O.C.D., Emeritus Professor of the Pontifical Theological Faculty "*Teresianum*" (Rome) and expert on St. Thérèse, often spoke about the four "chords" of the heart: that is, four kinds of love or charity that every man and woman lives and is called to live in a profound way. That is, we are all called to live out love as sons or daughters; as brothers or sisters; as a spouse; and as fathers or mothers. This is true from both an anthropological and a theological point of view. We are all sons and daughters of our parents, even if—by chance—we never had met them; in that case, one would probably retain his adoptive parents as his father and mother. We are all brothers and sisters of our blood-siblings or at least of our closest friends. Most men and women are called to marriage, and thus express their spousal love; and all men and women are called to be fruitful, either through biological offspring—I mean, children—or through some other means of paternity or maternity: for example, as teachers or with one's nieces and nephews, etc. The same must be said from a theological point of view: we are all sons and daughters of God; we are all brothers and sisters among us; we are all called to live a strong spousal relationship with God, and thus be soul-spouses for the Bridegroom, Christ. This spousal relationship with God brings forth, as a natural—or, I should say, supernatural—consequence, a spiritual fruitfulness. In other words, we are all called, as well, to become fathers or mothers of many souls, that is, spiritual children. In others words, we are (and are called to be) sons and daughters of our parents and sons and daughters of God; brothers and sisters among us; spouses, some in Christian marriage, all with God; fathers and mothers, perhaps biologically, certainly spiritually.

THÉRÈSE: "SPOUSE" (OF JESUS) AND "MOTHER" (OF SOULS)

Thérèse most certainly lived these four kinds of relationships with a particular intensity, both in a natural and especially in a supernatural way: daughter of God (think of her "Little Way"); sister (in her fraternal charity toward all); spouse (of Jesus); and mother (of many, many souls).

I believe that it was Thérèse's being a *spouse of Jesus*, in such a strong way, that led to her becoming a *mother of many souls*; I also am convinced that the Blessed Virgin Mary shared with her, in a special way, her spiritual maternity toward souls.

Before analyzing more closely her spiritual maternity, let's take just a few moments to examine her spousal relationship with Jesus. It is from this union with Jesus, her Spouse—the Spouse of the Church—that Thérèse's maternity stems.

One example will suffice. Actually, one phrase will suffice. And it's the following: "Jesus is my only love!" (*Jésus est mon unique Amour!*). Some scholars say that this phrase of Thérèse is a sort of synthesis of her entire spirituality. I agree. I would also add that—even if it were not to sum up all of her spirituality—it is certainly a summary of her spousal relationship with Jesus. Thérèse engraved this phrase—*Jésus est mon unique Amour!*—into the wood of the left-hand frame of the door of her cell.[1] It was the third and last cell she lived in, in the Lisieux Carmel (besides the Infirmary of course, in the last months of her life). She moved into her third cell in August of 1894, so certainly this inscription is subsequent to that date.[2] Fr. Pierre Descouvemont—one of the greatest scholars of Thérèse—retains that she probably wrote this phrase toward June of 1897, a few months before her death. We must remember that Thérèse was suffering terribly, not only physically, but also spiritually (and, consequently, psychologically). She was in the midst of her trial against faith: more specifically, the trial of faith in the existence of Heaven, as she confided to Pauline: "Ah! but I really believe in the Thief [= Jesus]! It's upon Heaven that everything bears. How strange and incomprehensible it is!" (CJ 7.2.3).[3] It was during

---

[1] Perhaps Thérèse was inspired, in this, by Deut 6:5–9, which was often read in the Liturgy of the Hours even in her time: "Love the Lord your God with all your heart and with all your soul and with all your strength. These commandments that I give you today are to be on your hearts. Impress them on your children. Talk about them when you sit at home and when you walk along the road, when you lie down and when you get up. Tie them as symbols on your hands and bind them on your foreheads. Write them on the doorframes of your houses and on your gates." See https://archives.carmeldelisieux.fr/en/oeuvres-de-therese/ecrits-divers/jesus-est-mon-unique-amour/ (accessed on April 1st, 2025).

[2] Cf. https://archives.carmeldelisieux.fr/en/oeuvres-de-therese/ecrits-divers/jesus-est-mon-unique-amour/ (accessed on April 1st, 2025).

[3] *Yellow Notebook*, 7.2.3 (July 2nd, 1897, third statement).

this time of intense spiritual darkness and struggle (from Easter 1896 till her very death) that Thérèse made some bold and surprising gestures of faith. For example, she wrote the Creed in her own blood. And, in June of 1897, she scribbled on a scrap piece of paper: "My God, with the help of your grace, I am ready to shed all my blood for each of the articles of the Symbol" (Creed). Probably in the same time period, June of 1897, she also wrote this synthetic and powerful statement, carving it into the wood of her door-frame: *Jésus est mon unique Amour!* It's one of those things that Thérèse should not have done, according to the rules of the monastery. But she did it anyway. Such was her love for Jesus, her Spouse, her *unique Amour*.

THÉRÈSE'S "MATERNAL" CHARITY: HER FIRST EXPERIENCES

After this example of Thérèse's spousal love for Jesus, summed up in her phrase, *Jésus est mon unique Amour!*, let's now examine her maternal charity toward others. Which, again, is a consequence of her love and union for and with Jesus.

Thérèse is very explicit in calling a certain notorious sinner her "first child." I'm referring to the murderer Henri Pranzini. This "pregnancy," as it were—in a spiritual sense of the term—and "birth" of her first child, into Heaven, has a premise, or rather an important occurrence in Thérèse's life. It's the day of her "complete conversion," as she defined it in the *Story of a Soul*. I'm referring to the grace received on Christmas Eve of 1886. Thérèse was thirteen years old. I'm not going to recount the episode, evoked previously. "Thérèse was no longer the same," she would later write, "Jesus had changed her heart!" (cf. Ms A, 44v°–45v°). And she continued: "I felt *charity* enter into my soul, and the need to forget myself and to please others; since then I've been happy!" In the very next sentence, Thérèse starts to narrate her spiritual zeal for souls: "One Sunday, looking at a picture of Our Lord on the Cross [...], I was resolved to remain in spirit at the foot of the Cross and to receive the divine dew. I understood I was then to pour it out upon souls" (Ms A, 45v°). It was then that she heard about Pranzini, destined to the guillotine. "I wanted at all costs to prevent him from falling into hell, and to attain my purpose I employed every means imaginable" (cf. ibid.), Thérèse recounts; and she continues: "He had mounted the scaffold and was preparing to place his head in the formidable opening, when suddenly, seized by an inspiration, he turned, took hold of the *crucifix* the priest was holding out to him and *kissed* the *sacred wounds three times!*" (Ms A, 46r°). The "lips of my *'first child' were* pressed to the sacred wounds!" (Ms A, 46v°), Thérèse concludes. She then turns to an even wider horizon, stating, "After this unique grace my desire to save souls grew each day"; and she continues, writing,

> It was a true interchange of love: to souls I was giving the *blood of Jesus*, to Jesus I was offering these same souls refreshed by the *divine dew*. I slaked His thirst and the more I gave Him *to drink*, the more the thirst of my poor little soul increased, and it was this ardent thirst He was giving me as the most delightful drink of His love (ibid.).

Just after telling of the "grace of leaving my childhood," as she defined it, Thérèse passes on to the recounting of her "first child," Pranzini. This experience was for her not only that of a "spiritual maternity." This "first child," as well as many other souls, was "born" precisely out of the "true interchange of love" between Jesus and Thérèse—a spousal love, that generated children, spiritual children. As regards to Pranzini, Céline Martin (Sr. Geneviève of the Holy Face) would later testify:

> The Servant of God used to call Pranzini "her child." Later, in Carmel, whenever she received some money on her feastday, she used to get Mother Prioress's permission to use it to get a Mass said. She would then whisper to me: "It's for my child; he must need it after all he's done. I must not abandon him now." After this memorable victory [in her adolescence, of Pranzini's conversion], Thérèse's zeal spread like a forest fire.

> She undertook to convert a woman who sometimes came to work for us, a complete heathen. She also instructed two poor girls in the faith. It was delightful to listen to her talking about God, and the children listened to her with rapt attention. Later, in Carmel, I saw her furtively slip some medals into the overcoats of the workers as they left the convent.[4]

THÉRÈSE'S CHARITY: BEYOND ANY CATEGORY

As we can tell from this testimony, Thérèse's fraternal charity was not limited to any category. This study has focused so far on some categories toward whom Thérèse exercised fraternal charity: her family members, sinners, priests, etc. These seemed the most significant, in my opinion, as groups of persons. However, Thérèse demonstrated her charity toward all those whom she had contact with, and—as we've seen and will see—toward many whom she would never actually know personally in her earthly life: sinners, priests, etc.

In fact, Thérèse evokes the canonical examination, preceding her Profession, when she declared what had brought her to Carmel: "I had declared at the feet of Jesus-Victim, in the examination preceding my profession, what I had come to Carmel for: 'I came to save souls and especially to pray for priests'" (Ms A, 69v°). Her sister Céline (Sr. Geneviève of the Holy Face) specified years later that in the canonical examination before one's Profession, each nun answered freely regarding the motives of their entrance into Carmel. So Thérèse's response to "save souls" and "especially to pray for priests" was all hers, according to Céline.

THÉRÈSE'S "MATERNAL" CHARITY TOWARD PRIESTS AND SINNERS

In Thérèse's correspondence with Céline, the categories of priests and sinners were especially dear. For Thérèse, it was in praying for priests that one could help sinners in a

---

[4] See O'Mahony, ed., *St. Thérèse of Lisieux by Those who Knew Her*, 129, 131.

special way. Priests were the missionaries, the soldiers in the spiritual battlefield for the salvation of souls; and her mission was to pray for them and assist them.[5] On August 15th, 1892, Thérèse wrote to Céline:

> It was one day when I was thinking of what I could do to save souls, a word of the Gospel gave me a real light [...]. Why, then, does Jesus say, "Ask the Lord of the harvest that he send some workers" [Mt 9:38]? Why?... Ah! it is because Jesus has so incomprehensible a love for us that He wills that we have a share with Him in the salvation of souls [...]. Our own vocation is not to go out to harvest the fields of ripe wheat. Jesus does not say to us: "*Lower* your eyes, look at the fields and go harvest them." Our mission is still more sublime. These are the words of our Jesus: "*Lift* your eyes and see" [Jn 4:35]. See how in my Heaven there are empty places; it is up to you to fill them, you are my Moses praying on the mountain, ask me for workers and I shall send them, I await only a prayer, a sigh from your heart!
>
> Is not the apostolate of prayer, so to speak, more elevated than that of the word? Our mission as Carmelites is to form evangelical workers who will save thousands of souls whose mothers we shall be... Céline, if these were not the very words of Jesus, who would dare to believe in them?... I find that our share is really beautiful, what have we to envy to priests? (LT 135).

"Thousands of souls whose mothers we shall be," Thérèse wrote to Céline. And indeed she was, mother of thousands—if not millions—of souls. A spiritual mother. A true mother.

AN "OLD" AND "NEW" VOCATION, AS EXPRESSED IN THÉRÈSE'S MANUSCRIPT B

Years later, in her *Manuscript* B, Thérèse would specify with great precision, in only a few phrases, what her vocation was; when writing spontaneously to Jesus on the six-year anniversary of her Profession (September 8th, 1896), she noted: "To be Your *Spouse*, to be a *Carmelite*, and by my

[5] Cf. *Prayer* 8, *Prayer for Abbé Bellière*, for example.

union with You to be the *Mother* of souls, should not this suffice me? And yet it is not so. No doubt, these three privileges sum up my true *vocation*: *Carmelite*, *Spouse*, *Mother*, and yet I feel within me other *vocations*" (Ms B, 2v°). And so Thérèse continued in her letter to Jesus, concluding with her famous phrase: "My vocation, at last I have found it . . . MY VOCATION IS LOVE! Yes, I have found my place in the Church and it is You, O my God, Who have given me this place; in the

THÉRÈSE IN A COMMUNITY PICTURE, EMBRACING THE CRUCIFIX IN THE COURTYARD OF THE MONASTERY (JUNE 1896: A FEW MONTHS BEFORE THÉRÈSE WROTE HER MANUSCRIPT B)

heart of the Church, my Mother, I shall be *Love*" (Ms B, 3v°).

It's worth noting that, for Thérèse, a "standard" or good Carmelite vocation is that of being a Spouse (of Jesus) and a Mother (of souls). (Note, also, that for Thérèse, being a mother is consequential to being a spouse: "To be Your *Spouse* [...], and by my union with You to be the *Mother* of souls," she wrote.) God, however, was attracting her to even wider horizons than an "average" Carmelite nun. She felt the vocation, as well, "of the WARRIOR, THE PRIEST, THE APOSTLE, THE DOCTOR, THE MARTYR" (Ms B, 2v°). Seeing that this was impossible to fulfill in a literal sense of the word, she found an answer in St. Paul's First Letter to the Corinthians: "And the Apostle explains"—Thérèse comments—"how all *the most PERFECT gifts* are nothing without *LOVE. That Charity is the EXCELLENT WAY that leads most surely to God*" (Ms B, 3v°). And so she concludes: "[I]n the heart of the Church, my Mother, I shall be *Love*. Thus I shall be everything, and thus my dream will be realized" (cf. ibid.).

THÉRÈSE'S POEMS: AN EXPRESSION OF HER "MATERNAL" CHARITY

Thérèse expresses this concept in her poetry as well. A couple of examples will suffice. In her poem for Céline (Sr. Geneviève of the Holy Face), *Poem* 24, in which she tries to encourage Céline not to focus on what she had given up for Jesus, but rather what He had given up for her, Thérèse wrote:

> Remember that your fruitful Dew
> Made the flowers' corollas virginal
> And made them able even in this world
> To give birth to a great number of hearts.
> I am a virgin, O Jesus! yet what a mystery.
> When I unite myself to You, I am the mother of souls.
> The virginal flowers
> Who save sinners,
> Remember (P 24).[6]

[6] Stanza 22 of *Poem* 24, *Jesus, My Beloved, Remember!*, in Kinney, transl., *The Poetry of Saint Thérèse of Lisieux*, 128.

For the feastday of her sister Pauline (Sr. Agnes of Jesus), on January 21st, 1897, Thérèse composed her *Poem* 45, *My Joy!* In handing it to her, she said: "My whole soul is in that [poem]."[7] In stanza 6, she wrote:

> My joy is to struggle unceasingly
> To bring forth spiritual children.
> It's with a heart burning with tenderness
> That I keep saying to Jesus:
> "For You, my Divine Little Brother,
> I'm happy to suffer.
> My only joy on earth
> Is to be able to please You" (P 45).

Thérèse depicts here, in this image, or "mirror," of her soul, something like a mother in birth-pangs. *"Ma joie, c'est de lutter sans cesse/ Afin d'enfanter des élus."* "My joy is to battle unceasingly, so as to give birth to the elect," is actually a more precise translation into English. It makes one think of the woman in the Book of Revelations, chapter 12, verses 1 and 2: "A great sign appeared in heaven: a woman clothed with the sun, with the moon under her feet and a crown of twelve stars on her head. She was pregnant and cried out in pain as she was about to give birth." Scholars say that this verse refers in the first place to the Church, our mother who cries out in pain as she gives birth to her children; and in the second place, to the Blessed Virgin Mary in giving "birth" to us, her spiritual children. However, in her *Poem* 45, Thérèse herself also identifies, in some way, with this woman struggling in her birth-pains.

TWO TELLING EPISODES FROM THÉRÈSE'S LIFE

To conclude this chapter on Thérèse's experience of spiritual maternity, let's take a look at just two more episodes from her life. The first regards her maternal love for sinners and for souls. In the Apostolic Process for Thérèse's canonization, Sr. Marie of the Trinity testified:

---

[7] See ibid., 184.

> She had a mother's love for souls and called them "her children." She thought of them continually and worked tirelessly to "gain their eternal life," as she put it. On a laundry day, I went to the laundry room in no hurry, examining the flowers in the garden as I passed. Sr. Thérèse of the Child Jesus was doing the same, but at a brisk pace; she soon caught up with me and said, dragging me along: "Is this the way to hurry when you have children to feed and have to work to support them? Let's hurry, because if we have fun, our children will starve."[8]

Thérèse demonstrated this same maternal attention and care also to the novices entrusted to her. Sr. Marie of the Trinity, because of her youth, had been forbidden to see Thérèse in the last months of her life, for fear that she, too, be infected with tuberculosis. She suffered very much from this distance from Thérèse, which had been imposed upon her (by the Prioress Mother Marie de Gonzague) through obedience. Fr. Pierre Descouvemont recounts in his book, *Thérèse of Lisieux and Marie of the Trinity*:

> [During her last months of sickness, Thérèse and Marie of the Trinity] met less often [...], but Thérèse showed her loving affection with even greater spontaneity. One day in June, Marie of the Trinity noticed the sick nun in her little wheelchair under the chestnut trees. Thérèse made a sign for her to come closer. "Oh! no," the novice answered her. "We will be seen and I don't have permission." And she went to cry in the hermitage of the Holy Face. How surprised she was after just a few moments to see Thérèse sitting next to her on a tree stump. *"I am not forbidden to see you,"* Thérèse said to her. *"Since I am dying, I want to console you."* Then laying the novice's head upon her

[8] See https://archives.carmeldelisieux.fr/en/naissance-dune-sainte/les-proces-la-sainte-de-therese/le-proces-apostolique/les-temoignages-du-proces-apostolique/#temoin-21-marie-de-la-trinite-et-de-la-sainte-face-o-c-d (accessed on April 1st, 2025). (I slightly revised this translation from French to English, after having consulted the original French version of Sr. Marie of the Trinity's testimony on the same Carmel of Lisieux Archives website.)

PHOTOGRAPH TAKEN THE DAY OF SR. MARIE OF THE TRINITY'S PROFESSION (APRIL 30TH 1896). From left to right: Sr. Martha of Jesus, Sr. Marie of the Sacred Heart (Marie Martin), Sr. Mary Magdalene, Sr. Mary of the Eucharist (Marie Guérin), and Thérèse. In the foreground, from left to right: Sr. Geneviève of the Holy Face (Céline Martin), Sr. Marie of the Trinity, and Mother Marie de Gonzague.

> heart, Thérèse began to wipe away her tears. And as Marie of the Trinity begged the sick nun—who was trembling with fever—to get back into her wheelchair, Thérèse replied to her: *"Yes, I'll get in, but not before you make me smile!"*[9]

Thérèse's maternal attitude is truly touching: it recalls that of Jesus and the beloved disciple John, who laid his head upon Jesus's heart in the Last Supper. Thérèse's affection and charity for Jesus alone—as she wrote on the wood of her door-frame, *Jésus est mon unique Amour!*—had purified and strengthened her charity toward all. This charity was to grow ever more in the last months of Thérèse's sickness, up until

[9] P. Descouvemont, *Thérèse of Lisieux and Marie of the Trinity: The Transformative Relationship of Saint Thérèse of Lisieux and her Novice Sr. Marie of the Trinity* (New York: Alba House, 1997), 36. His source was the CSM (*Conseils et Souvenirs de Marie*), no. 55.

the very last moment of her life. On September 30th, 1897, the last day of her life, Pauline (Sr. Agnes of Jesus) recorded Thérèse saying, in the midst of her anguishing physical and spiritual sufferings, that is, in her death agony and in her trial of faith, "Never would I have believed it was possible to suffer so much! Never! Never! I cannot explain this except by the ardent desires I have had to save souls" (CJ, September 30th).[10] Her last words, while looking at her crucifix: "Oh! I love Him! . . . My God . . . I love you! . . ." (ibid.).

10 *Yellow Notebook*, September 30th, 1897, in St. Thérèse of Lisieux, *Her Last Conversations*, transl. Clarke, 205.

NINTH CHAPTER

St. Thérèse's charity toward all men and women of all time

FOR A PREMISE: SOME THEOLOGICAL NOTIONS

The title of this last chapter is ambitious, if you think of it: St. Thérèse's charity toward all men and all women of all time. We'll see however, shortly, that this idea is not mine. It's Thérèse's. A charity that assumes such wide horizons is not something that can be born of the natural realm. "Flesh gives birth to flesh," Jesus tells Nicodemus in the Gospel of John, chapter 3, verse 6; "but the Spirit gives birth to spirit." Such a vast charity as that experienced and lived by Thérèse is clearly a gratuitous gift of God, a charism—I would say, a special and privileged participation in His charity. It is she who desired such wide, vast, and, I would say—to use a word dear to Thérèse—"infinite" horizons; but, clearly, this inspiration came from the Holy Spirit. Let's see how, briefly, but a bit more in detail.

Thérèse's charity toward all men and women of all time was a supernatural experience that matured in her during the entire course of her life, reaching its summit toward the end of her life. However, some premises of such a vast charity can be found even in her infancy and early years of life. A few examples will suffice.

EARLY SIGNS OF A VAST CHARITY

First of all, Thérèse herself attests to a divine call to religious life from her earliest years. To be precise, from her second year of age. She wrote:

> I had often heard it said that surely Pauline would become a *religious*, and without knowing too much about what it meant I thought: "I too *will be a religious*." This is one of my first memories and I haven't

> changed my resolution since then! It was through you, dear Mother, that Jesus chose to espouse me to Himself [...]. You were my *ideal*; I wanted to be like you, and it was your example that drew me toward the Spouse of Virgins at the age of two (Ms A, 6r°).

Although perceived in the mind and the consciousness of a two-year-old baby girl, and mediated through her childhood "ideal," Pauline, the calling to religious life was true. This is proven by the fact that such a calling remained in her heart her entire life, and—as Thérèse herself writes, after seven years of religious life—"This is one of my first memories and I haven't changed my resolution since then!"

Another sign of the Holy Spirit's action in Thérèse's soul at a precocious age is manifested in her mother Zélie's letters in which she mentions her baby girl. Thérèse quotes various of these letters. Her mother wrote to Pauline, on May 10th, 1877,

> Our two little dears, Céline and Thérèse, are angels of benediction, little cherubs. Thérèse is the joy and happiness of Marie and even her glory; it's incredible how proud she is of her. It's true she has very rare answers for one her age; she surpasses Céline in this who is twice her age. Céline said the other day: "How is it that God can be present in a small host?" The little one said: "That is not surprising, God is all-powerful" "What does all-powerful mean?" "It means He can do what He wants!" (Ms A, 10r°).

Thérèse was four years old when she spoke these words to Céline. Another incident in Thérèse's early age is very telling. Thérèse herself recounts this anecdote, again in the first pages of what she defined as a "Springtime story of a little white flower written by herself and dedicated to the Reverend Mother Agnes of Jesus" (Ms A, 2r°). We now call this text her *Manuscript* A. Thérèse wrote:

> One day, Léonie, thinking she was too big to be playing any longer with dolls, came to us with a basket filled with dresses and pretty pieces for making others; her doll was resting on top. "Here, my little sisters,

> *choose*; I'm giving you all this." Céline stretched out her hand and took a little ball of wool that pleased her. After a moment's reflection, I stretched out mine saying: "I choose all!" and I took the basket without further ceremony. Those who witnessed the scene saw nothing wrong and even Céline herself didn't dream of complaining (besides, she had all sorts of toys, her godfather gave her lots of presents, and Louise found ways of getting her everything she desired).
>
> This little incident of my childhood is a summary of my whole life; later on when perfection was set before me, I understood that to become *a saint* one had to suffer much, seek out always the most perfect thing to do, and forget self. I understood, too, there were many degrees of perfection and each soul was free to respond to the advances of Our Lord, to do little or much for Him, in a word, to *choose* among the sacrifices He was asking. Then, as in the days of my childhood, I cried out: "My God *'I choose all!'* I don't want to be a *saint by halves*, I'm not afraid to suffer for You, I fear only one thing: to keep my *own will*; so take it, for *'I choose all'* that You will!" (Ms A, 10r°–10v°).

This amusing episode from Thérèse's childhood helps us to understand how God was preparing her soul for an experience of totality: God wanted to pour out much love into Thérèse's heart, and so He made her desire—from her first years of life—"all." "I choose all," Thérèse had said; and when she had matured, she repeated this "I choose all." The totality of Thérèse's gift-of-self is a response to the totality of God the Father's gift of Himself, through Christ and in the Holy Spirit, to Thérèse. As St. John says in his First Letter, chapter 4, verse 10: "This is love: not that we loved God, but that he loved us and sent his Son as an atoning sacrifice for our sins." God loves us first; we respond to his love. And, in Thérèse's case, it is astonishing and moving to see how the Holy Spirit was at work in her soul from her first years of life.

THÉRÈSE'S EXPANDING CHARITY

The love of God, experienced in Thérèse's heart, soon manifested itself not only to her family members, but also to others. One example will suffice. It is again Thérèse who tells us of this episode that she lived as a child. She wrote:

> During the walks I took with Papa, he loved to have me bring alms to the poor we met on the way. On one occasion we met a poor man who was dragging himself along painfully on crutches. I went up to give him a coin. He looked at me with a smile and refused my offering since he felt he wasn't poor enough to accept alms. I cannot express the feeling that went through my heart. I wanted to console this man and instead I gave him pain or so I thought. The poor invalid undoubtedly guessed at what was passing through my mind, for I saw him turn around and smile at me. Papa had just bought me a little cake, and I had an intense desire to give it to him, but I didn't dare. However, I really wanted to give him something he couldn't refuse, so great was the sympathy I felt toward him. I remembered having heard that on our First Communion day we can obtain whatever we ask for, and this thought greatly consoled me. Although I was only six years old at this time, I said: "I'll pray for this poor man the day of my First Communion." I kept my promise five years later, and I hope God answered the prayer He inspired me to direct to Him in favor of one of His suffering members (Ms A, 15r°).

The grace of God was opening Thérèse's heart to all, although only a child: she writes of not being able to "express the feeling that went through my heart"; of her desire to "console this man" (who was a complete stranger to her); of an "intense desire" to give something (first a coin, and then a cake) to the poor man; of a "great [...] sympathy" toward him. In Thérèse's sensitive and compassionate nature, which God had endowed her with, the Holy Spirit was at work: with His gifts, He was making her virtues grow and expanding her soul on a supernatural level. Thérèse had said to herself, in fact,

"I'll pray for this poor man the day of my First Communion." And she remembered her promise.

"THÉRÈSE'S ZEAL SPREAD LIKE A FOREST FIRE"

I could go on, but our time is limited; we must skip forward in time to the end of Thérèse's life, at the summit of her maturity, so as to discover the fullness of her charity. We already heard Céline's testimony of how Thérèse directed her charity toward all whom she approached, and to all who approached her. She testified:

> The Servant of God used to call Pranzini "her child." Later, in Carmel, whenever she received some money on her feastday, she used to get Mother Prioress's permission to use it to get a Mass said. She would then whisper to me: "It's for my child; he must need it after all he's done. I must not abandon him now." After this memorable victory [in her adolescence, of Pranzini's conversion], Thérèse's zeal spread like a forest fire. She undertook to convert a woman who sometimes came to work for us, a complete heathen. She also instructed two poor girls in the faith. It was delightful to listen to her talking about God, and the children listened to her with rapt attention. Later, in Carmel, I saw her furtively slip some medals into the overcoats of the workers as they left the convent.[1]

Thérèse's attention, care, and zeal was thus directed toward all. Let's examine now, briefly, how this zeal slowly but surely expanded to embrace all men and women of all time. The first and perhaps the most significant text that must be mentioned is her *Manuscript* B, and, in particular, the letter that she wrote spontaneously to Jesus on September 8th, 1896, on the six-year anniversary of her Profession. (Although the passage is a bit long, it's worth calling to our attention.) Thérèse wrote:

> O my Jesus! what is Your answer to all my follies? Is there a soul more *little*, more powerless than mine?

---

[1] See O'Mahony, ed., *St. Thérèse of Lisieux by Those who Knew Her*, 129, 131.

> Nevertheless even because of my weakness, it has pleased You, O Lord, to grant my *little childish desires* and You desire, today, to grant other desires that are *greater* than the universe.
>
> During my meditation, my desires caused me a veritable martyrdom, and I opened the Epistles of St. Paul to find some kind of answer [...]. Without becoming discouraged, I continued my reading, and this sentence consoled me: "*Yet strive after* THE BETTER GIFTS, *and I point out to you a yet more excellent way.*" And the Apostle explains how all *the most* PERFECT *gifts* are nothing without LOVE. *That Charity is the* EXCELLENT WAY *that leads most surely to God.*
>
> I finally had rest. Considering the mystical body of the Church, I had not recognized myself in any of the members described by St. Paul, or rather I desired to see myself in them *all*. *Charity* gave me the key to my *vocation*. I understood that if the Church had a body composed of different members, the most necessary and most noble of all could not be lacking to it, and so I understood that the Church *had a Heart and that this Heart was* BURNING WITH LOVE. *I understood it was Love alone* that made the Church's members act, that if *Love* ever became extinct, apostles would not preach the Gospel and martyrs would not shed their blood. I understood that LOVE COMPRISED ALL VOCATIONS, THAT LOVE WAS EVERYTHING, THAT IT EMBRACED ALL TIMES AND PLACES ... IN A WORD, THAT IT WAS ETERNAL!
>
> Then, in the excess of my delirious joy, I cried out: "O Jesus, my Love ... my vocation, at last I have found it ... MY VOCATION IS LOVE!"
>
> Yes, I have found my place in the Church and it is You, O my God, Who have given me this place; in the heart of the Church, my Mother, I shall be *Love*. Thus I shall be everything, and thus my dream will be realized (Ms B, 3r°–3v°).

This passage of Thérèse's *Manuscript* B has been defined as the "magna carta" of her "Little Way," and, in a certain sense, of her doctrine. Pope Francis, in his recent Apostolic Exhortation, reminds us that "In the end, all that counts is love."[2] And he proposed this "key to her vocation" as the fundamental key for understanding her specific contribution, as a Doctor of the Church, for the Church and the world today. Thérèse here effectively describes her "vocation within her vocation," and points to love, charity, as comprising all vocations. Not only: her charity participates in that of God's: she wants to embrace all times and places, and to live out every vocation that a human being and a Christian can possibly live—to reach as many souls as possible. In love, that is, in charity, she finds a key to her vocation, and a possible and real way of living out her infinite desires.

THE MATURITY OF THÉRÈSE'S CHARITY

It's time to turn toward a conclusion now. In the *Yellow Notebook*, Pauline transcribes various signs and manifestations of this universal charity that Thérèse expressed in the last months of her life. Of course, Thérèse herself expressed this immensity of charity which she was experiencing, in June and July of 1897. She wrote, for example, "You know, O my God, I have never desired anything but to love You, and I am ambitious for no other glory. Your Love has gone before me, and it has grown with me, and now it is an abyss whose depths I cannot fathom" (Ms C, 34v°–35r°). Shortly before this, in the same manuscript, she had written:

> Just as a torrent, throwing itself with impetuosity into the ocean, drags after it everything it encounters in its passage, in the same way, O Jesus, the soul who plunges into the shoreless ocean of Your Love draws with her all the treasures she possesses. Lord, You know it, I have no other treasures than the souls it has pleased You to unite to mine; it is You Who entrusted these treasures to me, and so I dare to borrow the words You addressed to the Heavenly Father, the last night which saw You on our earth as a traveler and a mortal [...]:
>
> *"I have glorified you on earth; I have finished the work you gave me to do. And now do you, Father,*

---

[2] See Pope Francis, Apostolic Exhortation *C'est la confiance*, no. 50.

> *glorify me with yourself, with the glory I had with you before the world existed.*
>
> *"I have manifested your name to those whom you have given me out of the world. They were yours, and you have given them to me, and they have kept your word. Now they have learned that whatever you have given me is from you; because the words you have given me, I have given to them. And they have received them, and have known of a truth that I came from you, and they have believed that you sent me.*
>
> *"I pray for them, not for the world do I pray, but for those whom you have given me, because they are yours; and all things that are mine are yours; and yours are mine; and I am glorified in them. And I am no longer in the world, and I am coming to you. Holy Father, keep in your name those whom you have given to me"* (Ms C, 34r°–34v°).

Thérèse, in this passage, audaciously quotes and makes her own the priestly prayer of Jesus to the Father: "Holy Father, keep in your name those whom you have given to me."

Shortly after having written these words, among the last of her *Manuscript* C, Thérèse told Pauline something which she promptly transcribed in her *Yellow Notebook*:

> I feel that I'm about to enter into my rest. But I feel especially that my mission is about to begin, my mission of making God loved as I love Him, of giving my little way to souls. If God answers my desires, my Heaven will be spent in doing good on earth. This isn't impossible, since from the bosom of the beatific vision, the angels watch over us.
>
> I can't make Heaven a feast of rejoicing; I can't rest as long as there are souls to be saved. But when the angel will have said, "Time is no more!" then I will take my rest; I'll be able to rejoice, because the number of the elect will be complete and because all will have entered into joy and repose. My heart beats with joy at this thought (CJ, 7.17).[3]

[3] *Yellow Notebook*, July 17th (1897).

We must note, here, the eschatological tone of her discourse: her words almost seem to echo those of St. Paul in his first letter to the Corinthians, chapter 15, verses 26–28:

> The last enemy to be destroyed is death. For he "has put everything under his feet." Now when it says that "everything" has been put under him, it is clear that this does not include God himself, who put everything under Christ. When he has done this, then the Son himself will be made subject to him who put everything under him, so that God may be all in all.

The day after having pronounced those solemn and joyful words about the end of times and her intercession, from Heaven, for all souls until the number of elect will be complete, Thérèse adds, on July 18th: "God would not have given me the desire of doing good on earth after my death, if He didn't will to realize it; He would rather have given me the desire to rest in Him" (CJ 7.18.1).[4] Already a month before, on June 9th, Sr. Marie of the Sacred Heart (Marie Martin) told Thérèse that "we would be very sorry after she died." And Thérèse responded: "Oh! no, you will see . . . it will be like a shower of roses."[5] I could continue, but we must conclude this chapter. In the last months of her life, and even only a few days before her death, Thérèse continued to make promises about the good she would do after her death: on September 26th, her sister Céline testifies, "I said to her one day: 'You will look at us from up there in Heaven, right?' She replied spontaneously: 'No, I shall come down!'"[6]

---

[4] Ibid., July 18th.

[5] See the *Additional Conversations* transcribed by Sr. Agnes of Jesus (Pauline Martin), in St. Thérèse of Lisieux, *Her Last Conversations*, transl. Clarke, 256.

[6] O'Mahony, ed., *St. Thérèse of Lisieux by Those who Knew Her*, 228.

ST. THÉRÈSE OF LISIEUX (1896)

CONCLUSION

This spiritual journey that we have undertaken together to penetrate into Thérèse's burning charity toward God and toward neighbor has considered her fraternal charity from multiple points of view.

A glance at the two-fold Commandment that Jesus taught—love for God and for neighbor—reminded us that Thérèse herself purposefully based her own experience of fraternal charity precisely on this Commandment, as well as on Jesus's New Commandment to love one another as He has loved us. We then proceeded to delve into Thérèse's experience of fraternal charity in and toward her family. Having examined the "roots," as it were, of her fraternal charity—in the Martin family—allowed us to better appreciate Thérèse's fraternal charity toward other categories of persons, especially toward priests and sinners, the most privileged recipients of her ardent fraternal charity.

Thérèse's charity spread and grew, even reaching holy souls in Purgatory and the saints in Heaven, and later expanding itself to reach all men and women of all time ... The counter-proof of such a universal charity, however, is to be found in her day-to-day and "practical"—and, all the more so, heroic—charity toward the nuns in her monastery. Although young, Thérèse also demonstrated a unique charity toward her spiritual "sons and daughters," starting with the novices entrusted to her care.

Thérèse's message is timeless. And she speaks for herself. Yet, someone must "turn on a megaphone," as it were, so that her voice can be heard in the world today. My hope is that this study may be useful for "amplifying" Thérèse's voice in your heart and soul, and, in turn, that you also might speak of her message to your neighbor, not so much by words ... but rather by deeds.

BIBLIOGRAPHY

SOURCES OF ST. THÉRÈSE OF THE CHILD JESUS AND OF THE HOLY FACE

Les Cahiers d'école de Thérèse de Lisieux (1877–1888) [*The School Notebooks of Thérèse of Lisieux (1877–1888)*], introduction and notes by Msgr. Guy Gaucher in collaboration with the Carmel de Lisieux, Paris: Cerf, 2008.

I Testimoni di Teresa di Gesù Bambino dai Processi di Beatificazione e Canonizzazione, translated by Amata Ruffinengo, Rome: Edizioni OCD, 2004.

Procés de Béatification et Canonisation de Sainte Thérèse de l'Enfant-Jésus et de la Sainte-Face (I—Procès Informatif Ordinaire); *Procés de Béatification et Canonisation de Sainte Thérèse de l'Enfant-Jésus et de la Sainte-Face* (II—Procès Apostolique et petit procès pour la recherche des écrits de la sainte), Rome: Teresianum, 1973 and 1976.

Ste. Thérèse de l'Enfant-Jésus et de la Sainte-Face, *Œuvres complètes (Textes et Dernières Paroles)*, Lonrai: Éditions du Cerf/ Desclée De Brouwer, 1992.

St. Thérèse of Lisieux, *General Correspondence*, translated by John Clarke, O.C.D., 2 vols. (*1877–1890* and *1890–1897*), Washington, D.C.: ICS Publications, Washington, D.C. 1982–1988.

St. Thérèse of Lisieux, *Her Last Conversations*, translated by John Clarke, O.C.D., Washington, D.C.: ICS Publications, 1977.

Ste. Thérèse de l'Enfant-Jésus et de la Sainte-Face, *Édition critique des Œuvres Complètes, en huit volumes* [*Critical Edition of the Complete Works, in Eight Volumes*], 2nd edition, "Nouvelle Édition du Centenaire," Lonrai: Éditions du Cerf/Desclée De Brouwer, 1992.

Sr. Geneviève of the Holy Face, *My Sister Saint Thérèse (CSG)*, authorized translation by the Carmelite Sisters of New York of *Conseils et Souvenirs*, Rockford, Illinois: TAN Books and Publishers, 1992.

Story of a Soul. The Autobiography of Saint Thérèse of Lisieux, translated from the original manuscripts by John Clarke, O.C.D., a Study Edition prepared by Marc Foley, O.C.D., Washington, D.C.: ICS Publications, 2012.

St. Thérèse of Lisieux by Those who Knew Her: Testimonies from the Process of Beatification, edited by Christopher O'Mahony, Dublin: Veritas Publications, 1995.

Teresa di Lisieux, *Consigli e Ricordi*, Rome: Città Nuova Editrice, 1973. (The Italian version of Céline's *Conseils et Souvenirs.*)

The Plays of Saint Thérèse of Lisieux: "Pious Recreations," General Introduction by Guy Gaucher, O. C. D., translated by Susan Conroy and David J. Dwyer, Washington, D. C.: ICS Publications, 2008.

The Poetry of Saint Thérèse of Lisieux. Complete Edition. Texts and Introductions, translated by Donald Kinney, O. C. D., Washington, D. C.: ICS Publications, 1996.

The Prayers of Saint Thérèse of Lisieux, General Introduction by Guy Gaucher, O. C. D., translated by Aletheia Kane, O. C. D., Washington, D. C.: ICS Publications, 1997.

The Carmel of Lisieux Archives Website: https://archives.carmel-delisieux.fr/en/

STUDIES ON ST. THÉRÈSE OF THE CHILD JESUS AND OF THE HOLY FACE

Magisterium

The Apostolic Exhortation *C'est la confiance* of the Holy Father Francis on Confidence in the Merciful Love of God for the 150th Anniversary of the Birth of St. Thérèse of the Child Jesus and the Holy Face (October 15th, 2023): https://www.vatican.va/content/francesco/en/apost_exhortations/documents/20231015-santateresa-delbambinogesu.html

The Apostolic Letter of His Holiness Pope John Paul II, *Divini Amoris Scientia* (October 19th, 1997): https://www.vatican.va/content/john-paul-ii/en/apost_letters/1997/documents/hf_jp-ii_apl_19101997_divini-amoris.html

Monographs

De Meester, C., *The Power of Confidence: Genesis and Structure of the "way of spiritual childhood" of Saint Thérèse of Lisieux*, transl. by Susan Conroy, New York: Alba House, 1998.

Descouvemont, P., *Thérèse of Lisieux and Marie of the Trinity: The Transformative Relationship of Saint Thérèse of Lisieux and her Novice Sr. Marie of the Trinity*, New York: Alba House, 1997.

Descouvemont, P., *Thérèse de Lisieux et son prochain*, Paris: Les Éditions du Cerf, 2003.

Ermatinger, C., *St. Thérèse of Lisieux, Spouse and Victim*, Washington, D. C.: ICS Publications, 2010.

Gaucher, G., *Saint Thérèse of Lisieux: The Story of a Life*, San Francisco, CA: Ignatius Press, 2019.

Gaucher, G., *Sainte Thérèse de Lisieux (1873–1897). Biographie*, Paris: Les Éditions du Cerf, 2010.

Gaucher, G., *The Passion of Thérèse of Lisieux. 4 April–30 September 1897*, New York: The Crossroad Publishing Company, 1990.

González, L. J., *Teresa di Lisieux. Intelligenza emotiva e Counseling spirituale*, Edizioni O.C.D., 2019.

La Bible avec Thérèse de Lisieux, edited by Sr. Cécile, of the Carmel de Lisieux, and Sr. Geneviève, O.P., of the Monastery of Clairefontaine, Paris: Les Éditions du Cerf, 1990.

Les mots de Sainte Thérèse de l'Enfant-Jésus et de la Sainte-Face: Concordance générale établie par Soeur Geneviève, o.p., de Clairefontaine Soeur Cécile, o.c.d., du Carmel de Lisieux, Jacques Lonchampt, Les Éditions du Cerf, Lonrai (Orne) 1996.

Patrizi, M. E., *Il Patto segreto. L'amicizia mistica di san Massimiliano Kolbe e santa Teresa di Lisieux*, Rome: C.d.C. Editrice, 2008.

Sainte Thérèse de Lisieux. La vie en images, edited by P. Descouvemont, H. N. Loose, and D. Leprince, Paris: Cerf, 1995.

Spence, J., *Living the Little Way: Six Keys to the Spirituality of St. Thérèse*, Gastonia, NC: TAN Books, 2026.

Spence, J., *Un'esperienza sponsale con Dio: l'influsso di san Giovanni della Croce su santa Teresa di Lisieux* (tesi di dottorato), Rome: Pontificia Facoltà Teologica "*Teresianum*," Rome, 2020.

Thérèse et Lisieux, [*Photographies*: H. M. Loose; *Texte*: P. Descouvemont; *Présentation*: D. Leprince], Paris: Cerf, 1991.

Articles

Assailly, A., "Thérèse, sœur des hommes dans les épreuves," *Annales de Sainte Thérèse de Lisieux* 2 (1973), pp. 7–12.

"De nouveaux CSM [*Conseils et Souvenirs de Marie de la Trinité*] (no 31–57)," VT 77 (1980).

Gayral, L., "Une maladie nerveuse dans l'enfance de Sainte Thérèse de Lisieux," *Carmel* (1959), pp. 81–96.

Maître, J., *L'Orpheline de la Béresina. Thérèse de Lisieux (1873–1897)*, Paris: Cerf, 1996, pp. 194–202.

Patrizi, M. E., "'La mia vocazione è l'amore.' Sulla scia di Maria," *Rivista di Vita Spirituale* 6 (1997), pp. 753–62.

Patrizi, M. E., "P. Kolbe e la spiritualità di Santa Teresa di Gesù Bambino," *Rivista di Vita Spirituale* 53 (1999), pp. 188–209.

Patrizi, M. E., "S. Teresa di Lisieux: 'Nella Chiesa io sarò l'amore,'" *La Madonna delle Laste* 11 (1996), p. 11.

Spence, J., "Dio Padre nell'esperienza e nella teologia di santa Teresa di Lisieux: un segno di speranza per il mondo di oggi" ["God the Father in the Experience and the Theology of Saint Thérèse of Lisieux: A Sign of Hope for the World Today"], pp. 149–64, in Strzyz-Steinert L., ed., *Ripensare la teologia con santa Teresa di Lisieux. Atti del Seminario di approfondimento (Pontificia Facoltà Teologica Teresianum, Roma, 23–24 maggio 2024)*, Theologie der Spiritualität. Quellen und studien 14, Sankt Ottilien, Germany: EOS Verlag, 2025.

Spence, J., "Una memoria 'vivente': la rilettura di san Giovanni della Croce da parte di santa Teresa di Lisieux," *Teresianum* 70 (2019/2), pp. 583–607.

www.ingramcontent.com/pod-product-compliance
Lightning Source LLC
LaVergne TN
LVHW090611110826
845146LV00001B/338

* 9 7 9 8 8 9 2 8 0 1 8 6 7 *